PRAISE FOR MATT DOMO AND
EVERYBODY WINS

Everybody Wins challenges leaders to move beyond incremental change and provides a clear, actionable road map for reimagining how value is created in the digital age. This isn't just theory—it's practical guidance from someone who helped build AWS and has guided organizations of every size through fundamental transformation. Matt has always led with authenticity and integrity—qualities that shine through in this book—and I'm proud to call him both a colleague and a friend. For anyone serious about leading with courage and clarity in a time of rapid disruption, this is an indispensable read.

—SEAN BOYLE
COO, Omniva Technologies; former CFO, AWS

Having helped design and launch Google's product excellence framework, at global scale, I deeply appreciate the complexity of transforming global chaos into a sustainable and winning strategy for change. Matt Domo achieves this at an entirely different order of magnitude. He has created the product excellence playbook for the AI-native era—an effort that took us at Google a couple of years, millions of dollars, and considerable resources.

Domo offers a window into how his brilliant mind transforms the seemingly impossible task of AI adoption into a living and adaptable strategy with step-by-step execution plans. He elegantly shares his "zoom in, zoom out" strategic approach—undoubtedly the same lens that helped him cofound AWS, one of history's most transformative platforms.

For any leader navigating AI transformation, this book serves as both a compass and the ultimate road map.

—SARA ZARE
Polymath; Polyglot Entrepreneur; AI Investor; Former Global Lead of Product Excellence, Google

Matt Domo delivers a clear, actionable guide to digital and AI transformation—grounded in real-world experience and focused on what matters most: people, culture, and leadership. A must-read for any executive facing disruption, whether they know it or not.

—JASON BAUMGARTEN
Global Head, CEO, and Board Practice, Spencer Stuart

Matt's book is a master class in clarity for the future: immensely readable, rich with stories, and tons of practical wisdom for embracing innovation in an ever-evolving world. Matt is consistently recognized as one of the top technology leaders around, and for good reason. You'll love this brilliant blueprint for thriving amid disruption.

—NICK LARSON
Founder and Host, *Silicon Zombies* podcast

This book is a grand slam home run. Matt Domo writes with energy, clarity, simplicity, and vision. It's like he was inside my head as I dealt with trying to bring AI into my organization. This is high-quality nourishment for those on the AI journey.

—JOSEPH L. LENGYEL
General, USAF (retired); Former Joint Chief, National Guard Bureau

Matt Domo paints a visionary road map with vivid depth, illustrating how to navigate digital transformation and foster a culture of true innovation. He brilliantly develops and articulates proven strategies for every challenge along the way. With a strong focus on customer-centric visioning—his North Star approach—he empowers us to draw from past lessons while shaping a future of lasting impact. Visionaries spark groundbreaking ideas, but innovators like Matt Domo make those ideas a reality.

—ESTHER M. LEGANT
Head of Investor Relations, Fraunhofer Institute for Manufacturing Engineering and Automation IPA

Matt Domo brings clarity and urgency to one of the most pressing issues facing leaders today: digital transformation. In *Everybody Wins*, Matt offers more than a framework—he provides a road map for thriving in the age of agility. He combines his pioneering experience helping build Amazon Web Services (AWS) with his engaging leadership style to show us that digital change is not just about technology; it is about people, vision, and the courage to jump from the "burning platform" into the future.

What sets Matt apart is his ability to translate complexity into clarity. Whether coaching executives, shaping board-level strategy, or unpacking the human side of innovation … I have seen firsthand his ability to inspire leaders not only to understand disruption but to harness it.

This is an essential guide for leaders who refuse to be left behind. Read it with a pencil in hand—you'll want to underline the insights that spark both conviction and action.

—JEFFREY LACKEY
CEO, JKL Advisors; Host, *Growing Your Business with People*; Former Head of Global Resourcing and Talent Acquisition, Rolls-Royce; Former Vice President, Talent Acquisition, CVS Health

As a CEO building an AI-first company, *Everybody Wins* is the essential road map I wish I'd had from day one. Matt Domo shows leaders exactly how to build a winning strategy, delivering more clarity and actionable insight than a team of "tier 1" consultants. Hands down the best way for any executive to save the day when it comes to AI disruption.

—SEBASTIAN RIVAS
CEO, Andes STR; University of Chicago Booth School of Business 2021 Annual Edward L. Kaplan, '71, New Venture Challenge Winner

Matt Domo nails the critical gaps between traditional business models and the AI-driven future. *Everybody Wins: The Business Leader's Mission Possible Guide to AI Success* will have you critically assessing the depth of your digital strategy and racing to implement AI-powered solutions on your path to personal and professional success. As a leader in digital lending, where speed and agility are everything, I've leaned on Matt's guidance to transform our operations. Your status quo will be challenged, but as Matt points out, "In the raging river of today's business changes, people clutch onto the driftwood of control." This book is your guide to letting go and leaping forward.

—CALVIN USIRI
CTO/CPO, Ramani Corporation; Forbes Africa "30 Under 30" Winner

Domo's *Everybody Wins: The Business Leader's Mission Possible Guide to AI Success* is an easy-to-digest road map for digital transformation that turns complexity into action. He reminds us, "The magic of AI isn't that it replaces people. It's that it reorients people … And it creates space for more meaningful, impactful work," while also challenging us that "Comfort doesn't lead to breakthroughs. Vision does."

From anchoring every initiative in a business goal to embracing AI as a force multiplier, this book is a must-read for leaders across every sector ready to innovate with purpose.

—HEATHER BELLINO
CEO, Texas Advocacy Project

EVERYBODY WINS

MATT DOMO

EVERYBODY WINS

THE BUSINESS LEADER'S
MISSION POSSIBLE
GUIDE TO AI SUCCESS

Entrepreneur | Books

Published by Entrepreneur® Books, Charleston, South Carolina.
An imprint of Advantage Media Group.

Entrepreneur® Books is a registered trademark of Entrepreneur Media, LLC and used under license to Advantage Media Group.

Printed in the United States of America.

10 9 8 7 6 5 4 3 2 1

ISBN: 979-8-89701-000-4 (Paperback)
ISBN: 979-8-89701-001-1 (eBook)
ISBN: 979-8-89701-002-8 (Audiobook)

Library of Congress Control Number: 2026901340

Cover design by Matthew Morse.
Layout design by Megan Elger.

This custom publication is intended to provide accurate information and the opinions of the author in regard to the subject matter covered. It is sold with the understanding that the publisher, Entrepreneur® Books, is not engaged in rendering legal, financial, or professional services of any kind. If legal advice or other expert assistance is required, the reader is advised to seek the services of a competent professional.

Since 1977, Entrepreneur Media has been dedicated to inspiring, informing, and celebrating the innovators who drive business forward. Entrepreneur® Books, launched in 2024 through a partnership with Entrepreneur Media, continues that mission by helping business and thought leaders share their insights, experiences, and expertise through custom books. Opinions expressed by authors of Entrepreneur® Books are their own. To be considered for publication, please visit books.Entrepreneur.com.

To my sons, Aidan and Maddox.

May you always choose action over inaction and never fear the risks you take. Build the future you believe in.

To my mother, Ruthann.

Your lesson that anything is possible if you work hard enough is the foundation of every blueprint. I know you would be proud.

And finally, to you, the reader.

May we all continue to pay it forward.
Do one kind thing for someone else today.

CONTENTS

PART IV: DIRECTING THE CHANGE

PART V: EMBEDDING INNOVATION IN YOUR DNA

INTRODUCTION

WE ARE LIVING through one of the most consequential leadership moments in a generation. The pace of change has accelerated to a level that few could have anticipated, and the implications of that shift are rippling across every industry. AI, automation, cloud platforms, and connected data ecosystems have opened a new frontier in how we operate, serve, compete, and grow. Yet the tools themselves are not the defining factor. The defining factor is what leaders do with them.

Across boardrooms and leadership teams, there is a deep tension in our awareness that the world is moving faster, paired with the sense that decision-making has not kept pace. Organizations are investing heavily in digital tools but struggling to see returns in customer impact, employee productivity, or sustainable innovation. What many leaders are quietly grappling with is not just a knowledge gap about technology but a deeper question about how to lead transformation in a way that creates clarity, momentum, and belief.

This book was written to respond to this moment. It offers a practical framework for leaders who are committed to growth but unsure how to navigate the complex landscape of digital change. It is designed to turn aspiration into action by providing a clear, actionable path forward. It is grounded in the real-world experiences of organizations that have redefined themselves not through massive disruption but through a series of disciplined, human-centered decisions that have reshaped how work gets done.

There is a profound opportunity available right now for leaders who choose to engage with it. The companies that are winning in this environment are those that treat transformation as a continuous capability. They create cultures in which experimentation is rewarded, data informs direction, and people feel trusted to move with speed and autonomy. These are achievable practices that begin with behaviors modeled at the top.

If you are a leader who sees both the urgency and the opportunity of this moment, then this book was written for you. It is your blueprint, but more than anything, it is a message of possibility for you, for your team, and for the future you are building.

My Journey from Cloud Pioneer to Transformation Architect

My path into technology did not begin with a plan to shape the future of business or contribute to one of the most disruptive platforms in history. It began with curiosity. I wanted to understand how systems worked, how people made decisions, and why some ideas scale while others stall. That curiosity eventually brought me to Amazon during a moment of profound experimentation. I joined the founding team that built Amazon Web Services (AWS), a simple concept that evolved into the backbone of the modern digital economy.

Those early years at AWS shaped my worldview. We were not building a set of tools. We were designing an entirely new operating model for how ideas become real. We learned to move with speed, to test relentlessly, and to embrace the discipline of working backward from the customer. Every breakthrough came from clarity of purpose and a willingness to rethink what was possible. That experience showed me that transformation is not an act of ambition but a system of behavior that can be designed, taught, and scaled.

After helping launch AWS globally, I had the opportunity to partner with leaders across industries who were navigating seismic change. I worked with Fortune 500 companies wrestling with legacy complexity, startups pushing the boundaries of what comes next, universities shaping the next generation of talent, and governments modernizing national infrastructures. In every setting, the pattern remained consistent: Technology alone does not transform an organization. Transformation happens when leadership, culture, and systems evolve together.

I wrote this book after seeing too many leaders burdened by complexity that does not need to exist. They are surrounded by experts speaking in acronyms and abstractions, yet what they truly need is clarity. They need a way to connect strategy to execution, systems to outcomes, and people to purpose. Transformation should feel like progress, not chaos. I want to demystify transformation and return confidence to leadership. As such, every chapter of this book is built to make action achievable. Every idea serves a single aim: to help you lead with clarity, courage, and conviction. Progress becomes inevitable when the path forward is structured, human-centered, and grounded in principle. Just remember along the way that the future belongs to leaders who build with intent and who choose to shape change rather than react to it.

THE OPPORTUNITY WHERE EVERYBODY WINS

For years, the term *digital transformation* has been mischaracterized as a technical initiative. It has been treated as a platform upgrade, a cloud migration, or a set of tools deployed to bring an organization up to speed. But at its core, transformation means unlocking human and business potential at scale. It is the discipline of designing systems, workflows, and strategies that elevate how people work, how value is created, and how impact is sustained.

This book is grounded in a belief that transformation can and should serve everyone it touches. That belief is embodied in a concept I call the ME Experience—or MEx. MEx is the connective tissue between vision and value. It asks a powerful and often overlooked question: What does transformation feel like to the person experiencing it? When you prioritize the ME in every equation (the customer ME, the employee ME, the leader ME), you ensure that change is not just implemented but internalized. And when people feel the benefit of change directly, they carry its momentum forward.

For the customer, MEx means designing products and services that are intuitive, responsive, and grounded in real needs—eliminating friction, delivering value faster, and creating moments that feel thoughtful, not transactional. For the employee, MEx means removing the barriers that make work harder than it needs to be while equipping people with tools that support flow, agency, and clarity so they can contribute with confidence and grow with purpose. For the leader, MEx is the shift from directing change to enabling it. It is the practice of communicating clearly, modeling desired behaviors, and creating space for innovation to thrive.

When transformation is built around these principles, everyone moves forward. Customers stay longer because they feel understood. Employees engage more deeply because they feel empowered. Organizations grow more resilient because they can adapt without chaos. This is the triple-win model at the heart of modern leadership: When done right, transformation is not a trade-off between efficiency and empathy, or scale and speed. It is a strategy where everybody wins.

The future is not just digital; it is personal. When you lead through that lens, you elevate the experience of everyone inside it. This book is your road map to building that kind of system, where human-centered design, operational excellence, and leadership clarity converge.

What This Book Is ... and Isn't

Before we go any further, let me be clear about what this book is *and* what it is not.

This is not a buzzword manual. You won't find pages filled with jargon or empty platitudes. There's already enough noise in the world of digital transformation, and too much of it has created confusion instead of clarity. This book doesn't aim to impress with trendy terminology. It aims to equip you with language that lands, stories that resonate, and guidance that translates directly into action.

This is not a technical guide. You don't need to be a software engineer, data scientist, or AI expert to lead transformation. This book assumes you are a leader, not a systems architect. And while technology is a central part of the story, it is not the protagonist. The real focus here is on how leaders shape the environment for change—how they communicate, how they structure teams, how they model behavior, and how they build momentum across the business.

This is also not another theoretical book on transformation that sounds compelling in a keynote but fails to create movement on the ground. Too many strategy decks end up collecting dust. Too many "big ideas" never make it past the whiteboard.

So, what *is* this book?

It is a practical playbook for leaders who want to move from intention to execution. Every chapter includes frameworks you can apply, stories that illustrate real outcomes, and tools you can start using with your teams immediately. You'll find checklists, diagnostics, and decision models built for action, not simply reflection.

It's also a confidence builder. Transformation can be daunting, especially when the pace of technology feels relentless and the pressure to get it right is high. I wrote *Everybody Wins* to help you navigate the complexity, remove the guesswork, and lead change in a way that feels tangible, human, and possible. My goal is to help you lead with more clarity, more conviction, and more capability, because transformation is a mission every leader can drive.

How to Use This Book

Everybody Wins is not designed to be read once and shelved, so mark it up, revisit, and apply. Whether you're leading a company-wide transformation or simply trying to bring more clarity and speed to your own team, the structure of this book is designed to meet you where you are and move with you.

The book is organized into five parts, each one tackling a core component of transformation—why it matters, how it starts, and how to sustain it across your organization.

Part I: The Digital Imperative begins by grounding you in context. It explores what's changed in the business landscape, why traditional approaches are no longer sufficient, and what this moment demands of modern leaders. This section is your why—a way to make sense of the urgency and opportunity ahead.

Part II: Leading the Charge shifts the focus to leadership. This section is about building the courage, communication skills, and conviction to lead transformation with clarity. It introduces practical ways to close the say–do gap, activate your teams, and create cultural alignment from the top down.

Part III: Powering Up for Transformation explores how to use tools and technology with intention. This is not a tech spec section but a set of strategies for bringing digital platforms to life in a way that serves customers, empowers employees, and delivers measurable business value. You'll learn how to integrate AI, analytics, and automation into your operations without losing the human element that drives real change.

Part IV: Directing the Change is where we shift into operating reality. You'll explore how to redesign workflows, decision-making processes, and organizational structures to unlock speed, adaptability, and focus. This section is about putting transformation on rails so it doesn't stall, get stuck, or lose its way.

Part V: Embedding Innovation in Your DNA addresses the long game. It's one thing to spark transformation. It's another to sustain it. Here, we look at how to embed learning, experimentation, and momentum into the fabric of your organization so innovation becomes a habit, not a headline.

At the beginning of each chapter, you'll find a Mission Possible Blueprint. These are tactical summaries designed to convert insight into action. And at the end of each chapter are Five Steps to Take Now sections. Think of them as your quick-reference guides, tools to help you run better meetings, ask sharper questions, make smarter decisions, and build buy-in across your team.

You can read this book cover to cover or dive into the section that aligns with where you're feeling the most friction right now. However you choose to approach it, this book is here to give you the tools, stories, and structure to lead the transformation you know is possible.

This Is Your Mission Possible

Every leader I've worked with—regardless of industry, title, or tenure—has asked some version of the same question: *Can I really do this?* Not just survive a wave of digital change, but lead it. Shape it. Use it as a catalyst for something better.

The answer, unequivocally, is yes.

This book exists to show you that transformation is not reserved for the tech elite. It's not the exclusive domain of software startups or innovation labs. It is a leadership discipline, available to anyone willing to think deeply, move decisively, and commit to the work of change. That includes *you*.

Your mission, should you choose to accept it, is not just to modernize your organization. It's to make it faster, wiser, more connected, and more human. That starts with how you lead. The words you choose. The priorities you reinforce. The moments you make space for growth instead of fear. When you model the shift, others follow.

In the pages ahead, I'll offer frameworks and tactics, but more importantly, I'll share the truths behind what actually moves the needle. The moments where leaders stepped into uncertainty and found clarity. The systems they reimagined. The metrics they changed. And the signals they sent when they celebrated learning over perfection.

You'll meet teams who delivered new experiences faster, not because they had better tools, but because they had better alignment. You'll see how frontline employees became innovation engines, how friction turned into momentum, and how culture became the ultimate accelerant.

What I ask of you is simple: Don't just read this book. Use it. Start the conversations. Run the experiments. Ask the uncomfortable questions. Challenge the status quo with humility and purpose. And above all, believe that meaningful transformation is not only possible but within reach, starting right now.

So take a breath. Lean in. And get ready to lead with clarity, courage, and conviction.

This is your mission possible. Let's begin.

PART I

THE DIGITAL IMPERATIVE

CHAPTER ONE

THE BURNING PLATFORM

Why Digital Transformation Is No Longer Optional

If you don't like change, you're going to like irrelevance even less.
—GENERAL ERIC SHINSEKI,
FORMER US ARMY CHIEF OF STAFF

Your Mission Possible Blueprint: The burning platform is real, and the opportunity is massive. By the end of this chapter, you'll understand exactly why waiting is the riskiest digital strategy of all, and you'll have five specific actions you can take this week to begin your transformation journey.

IF SOMEONE HAD told me back in the early 2000s that I'd one day be known for helping to sell air, I probably would've laughed. But in a very real sense, that's exactly what our team did when we built Amazon Web Services (AWS). And as wild as that sounds, AWS laid the foundation for what became one of the most transformative business models in modern history.

To set the stage, you have to understand what technology infrastructure looked like in the late 1990s and early 2000s. It was a game of expensive guesswork. Companies had to predict their growth—six, nine, even twelve months out—and make massive capital investments in physical hardware: servers, storage, networking, and data center space. If they guessed wrong, they either overbuilt and hemorrhaged money or underbuilt and couldn't scale fast enough to meet demand. There was no flexibility. There was no room for agility. Businesses rose or fell on the accuracy of their forecasts.

Inside Amazon, we were growing rapidly and facing those same challenges. We realized we needed to find a better way to scale. So we began investing heavily in automation—removing manual steps wherever we could, replacing fragile workflows with reliable, repeatable ones. This wasn't about cutting corners; it was about enabling speed, simplicity, and control at scale. And slowly, we began to realize something: If this invisible infrastructure worked for us, why couldn't it work for others?

So we made the leap. We began building something entirely new. Not a product that customers could hold in their hands but a *service* they could call into existence with on-demand computation, storage, and database power delivered over the internet. To a lot of people, this sounded ridiculous. "Renting servers over the internet?" I can't count how many times I heard that exact phrase. "Who's going to trust something they can't see or touch?"

But we weren't building this because it sounded trendy. We were solving a real problem—one we had lived ourselves. And what we saw on the other side was crystal clear: the ability to move fast, test ideas quickly, manage costs more precisely, and focus resources on what really mattered—the customer.

Still, we faced plenty of resistance, even internally. People thought we were crazy. "You're going to fail," they said. "This is too hard, too risky." And I understood where that fear came from. In times of rapid change, people cling to what they know. I always say this: In the raging river of today's business changes, people clutch onto the driftwood of control. They say, "I own this. What can you possibly teach me? It works just fine, go away!" But comfort doesn't lead to breakthroughs. Vision does.

Comfort doesn't lead to breakthroughs. Vision does.

So we did what any good product builder does: We told stories. We painted a picture of what was possible. We showed how cloud computing could free teams from the weight of capex-heavy infrastructure, from racking and stacking servers, from waiting months for provisioning and approvals. Instead of raising millions to build the foundation of your app, now you could swipe a credit card and be live in minutes. Instead of maintaining massive server rooms, you could focus on building features your customers cared about.

One of our first major customers was Twitter. I remember asking, "What's a tweet?" I had no idea what they were talking about. But we worked closely with them, and with dozens of other startups, to refine the service. And over time, the message started to resonate. Agility. Simplicity. Control. Predictability. We weren't selling air—we were selling the ability to move, pivot, and grow with confidence.

Looking back, what we created was more than a cloud platform. It was a shift in mindset. It was about making infrastructure as simple and invisible as possible, just like the Amazon retail experience—recommendations, personalization, and ease. If Amazon could suggest glasses for your whiskey when you add ice molds to your cart, why couldn't we help companies see the value of connecting one innovation to another? Why couldn't we create tailwinds for their success, just as we had created ours?

And we did. From 2017 to 2024, AWS grew from $17.4 billion in annual revenue to more than $107.5 billion, making it the most profitable segment of Amazon's business.[1] That kind of growth came from real, sustained value delivered to organizations around the globe.

Beyond the numbers, the most important lesson I learned was this: Sometimes the most transformational opportunities are hiding in plain sight. They're in the systems people take for granted. They're in the inefficiencies people stop noticing. They're in the invisible scaffolding of how work gets done.

I learned that you have to be willing to ask, What if we started over? or Is there a way we can make this easier, simpler, and more reliable? to explore new ways of enabling customers and empowering employees. You have to be willing to step into the uncertainty because the future is *yours to shape.*

Sometimes the most transformational opportunities
are hiding in plain sight.

---

1   "Amazon Web Services Revenue 2014–2024," *Statista*, accessed April 18, 2025, https://www.statista.com/statistics/233871/amazon-web-services-revenue/.

The Burning Platform

In 1988, a worker was trapped on an oil platform in the North Sea when it caught fire. The inferno was raging. His options were bleak: stay where he was and be consumed by flames or jump fifteen stories into icy, uncertain waters. Either choice came with risk. But staying put guaranteed destruction. So he jumped. That terrifying leap into the unknown became a symbol for the kinds of decisions many leaders are facing today.[2] And that's exactly where most organizations sit when it comes to digital transformation.

The thing is, in business, the "platform" doesn't always *look* like it's burning. On the surface, things might seem stable. Business is still happening. Revenue is still coming in. You might even be hitting this quarter's targets. But underneath, the conditions are rapidly changing. Customers are evolving faster than most businesses. In fact, we've officially reached the age when it's all about *me, me, me*—something I refer to as ME or MEx (ME experience). Because today's customers expect experiences that are simple, easy, frictionless, and hyperpersonalized, delivered exactly when, where, and how they want them. This expectation now stretches across every touchpoint a customer has with your brand. The question leaders must ask is, How do we make MEx successful on first contact, at every step of their journey, and in a way that's meaningful to what matters most to them? This strategy is not about serving people's self-centered interests but about serving *people*. When organizations design around individual consumer needs rather than internal organizational convenience, breakthrough results follow.

This paradigm doesn't stop with the customer; it also applies equally to the internal MEx—that is, your employees. Just as external

---

2   "Survivor Jumped 174ft to Escape Fireball," *The Herald*, March 11, 1989, https://www.heraldscotland.com/news/11891591.survivor-jumped-174ft-to-escape-fireball/.

customers expect personalized, frictionless experiences, internal users need systems that adapt to their roles, reduce their friction, and amplify their impact. If we are committed to optimizing the external user experience (UX), we must also design employee workflows and systems that are just as seamless, empowering, and intuitive. That means eliminating tedious, time-consuming tasks and enabling employees to focus on higher-value work, whether that's innovation, collaboration, or customer engagement. Too often, businesses force both customers and employees to conform to outdated, internally focused processes. But organizations that invert that logic, designing around the needs of MEx rather than the convenience of the provider, achieve breakthroughs faster and with greater impact.

Additionally, competitors—especially digital-native ones—are adapting in real time. The pace of innovation is accelerating. And many of the models that once served us well are becoming dangerously outdated.

But because the pain isn't immediate, many leaders freeze. They hold on tighter to what they know, what feels safe. "We've always done it this way." "It's worked for years." "We'll get to digital when we have more time, more budget, less risk." I've heard every version of this from boardrooms and executive suites across industries—from global media companies to higher education institutions, to print publishers clinging to event revenue while their audiences migrate online.

That's the driftwood I mentioned earlier. When the current gets rough, people grab what's familiar. Or, often, they delay transformation, not out of comfort with the familiar or even out of ignorance, but because they are more focused on optimizing what they already have. Incremental improvements feel safer and easier to implement, and they directly address short-term pain points or operational concerns. But this mindset, while understandable, can become a trap.

It prioritizes internal efficiency over external impact, and stability over relevance. What's often missed is the imperative to shift focus toward a truly delighting MEx when expectations are changing faster than internal systems can evolve. The organizations that thrive are those that recognize incrementalism alone isn't enough; real transformation starts by re-centering value around the people they serve.

Let's look at what's really going on. The way customers engage with businesses has fundamentally shifted. People expect more. They want it now. They want it personalized. And they want it to be effortless. They don't want to jump through hoops to buy, to get support, to receive updates. They want intelligent, anticipatory service. And when they don't get it, they churn. They disengage. They find someone else who does it better.

Case in point: I worked with a multibillion-dollar entertainment company, one you've definitely heard of. When I walked in to talk about AI, the reaction was typical: "What are you going to tell me that I don't already know? I've been doing this for thirty-five years." And yet, their attendance was declining. Audience engagement was flatlining. Promotions weren't working. But they couldn't see why.

So we dug into the data. We looked at engagement trends, ad performance, offer timing, customer segmentation. What we found were clear, actionable patterns. The problem wasn't their product—it was the delivery, the timing, the lack of personalization. Once we tailored promotions to where and how customers actually interacted with them, results started to climb. But they had to let go of "we've always done it that way" to get there.

The breakthrough wasn't a onetime fix. We built ongoing monitoring systems that continue to surface new patterns and opportunities. This is the hallmark of modern transformation—not just solving today's problems but creating systems that continuously evolve your understanding of what's possible.

And that's really the point of this metaphor. The platform doesn't have to be engulfed in flames for the jump to be necessary. The future is demanding different things from your business. And if you wait until you're forced to change, you may not have enough runway left to catch up.

The future is demanding different things from your business.

Digital transformation, when you strip away the buzzwords, is about reimagining how you deliver value. It's rethinking *what* you offer, *how* customers experience it, and *how* your organization operates behind the scenes to deliver it. That might mean redesigning business processes, moving to value-based services, shifting to recurring revenue, or building entirely new models. But the thread running through all of it is this: Make things simpler, easier, more relevant, and more human for your customer.

Now, I know this can feel overwhelming. You might be asking, Where do I even start? That's what this book is here to help with. We're not going to eat the elephant in one bite. We'll take it piece by piece, step by step—showing you how to identify the high-impact opportunities and execute them with confidence.

The key is to stop thinking of transformation as something you do *to* the business. It's something you do *with* the business—starting with the needs of your customers and your employees. Then you layer in the right technologies, the right processes, and the right leadership mindset to get there.

The key is to stop thinking of transformation as something you do to the business. It's something you do with the business— starting with the needs of your customers and your employees.

Because staying where you are might seem safe, but in a market defined by speed, agility, and experience, it's often the riskiest move of all. The jump may feel daunting. But what's on the other side? That's where the real opportunity lives.

Disruption as a Growth Lever: How AI and Emerging Tech Unlock New Models

When people hear the word *disruption*, their minds often go straight to the negative. Layoffs. Market cannibalization. Industry extinction. But I want to reframe that for you, because disruption isn't inherently destructive. When you approach it with the right mindset, disruption becomes a growth lever. It becomes a catalyst for innovation, simplification, and value creation.

AI is a big part of that picture. But it's not the whole picture. Digital transformation isn't about one shiny technology. It's about how we use a constellation of emerging tools, such as AI, automation, data analytics, and intelligent systems, to fundamentally change how value is created and delivered. And it's about changes in the business model and ways the business delivers value within the model.

The magic of AI isn't that it replaces people. It's that it *reorients* people. It clears the clutter. It removes friction. And it creates space for more meaningful, impactful work.

I've worked with law firms where junior attorneys would spend weeks building briefs—tedious, manual, and mentally exhausting.

And yes, that was one of the ways they learned the law. But what if, instead of starting from scratch, they could begin 80 percent of the way there? What if generative AI could create the first draft in minutes—one that still needed human review and input, but saved hours of research and formatting? Suddenly, that junior attorney has time to refine the facts and change the narrative for the best outcomes for clients. That's a career accelerated.

Or take marketing. I once helped a nonprofit leadership team whose members dreaded writing their strategic plan. It was all in their heads, but the thought of getting it on paper felt overwhelming. So we used AI to turn a simple interview into a first draft. Then we refined it together. What should've taken weeks took hours.

Here's the shift in mindset I want leaders to make: Efficiency isn't the enemy of employment. It's the enabler of empowerment. When we talk about automating repetitive tasks, we're not talking about eliminating jobs—we're talking about *freeing people* to do the work that actually moves the needle. Too often, I see organizations fall into the "efficiency equals elimination" trap. They hear "automate," and they start drawing up pink slips. That's not innovation—that's short-termism. Real innovation is what happens when you ask, What could my team do if it wasn't buried under repetitive processes? What new services could we offer? Which markets could we enter? How much faster could we serve our customers? In what ways could we add greater value to MEx? AI is a growth multiplier, not a workforce reducer.

Efficiency isn't the enemy of employment.
It's the enabler of empowerment.

This is where disruption becomes transformative.

In real estate, for instance, the average home sale process involves more than thirty manual steps—forms, inspections, approvals, documentation handoffs. It's a mess. But imagine a workflow where those steps are automated, where approvals are triggered dynamically, where documents flow securely and seamlessly. Now the agent isn't stuck chasing paperwork; they're advising clients, closing deals, and growing the business. That's disruption with a capital *D*, and it's happening right now.

Let's go even further. Think about financial planning. Midsize companies often take two months to prepare their quarterly P&L statements, wrangling data from multiple departments, cleaning spreadsheets, building models. What if that process could be reduced to eight minutes with robotic process automation and machine learning? What if you could spot trends, deviations, and opportunities in near real time? Suddenly, you're not reacting to last quarter's numbers. You're shaping *this quarter's, this week's, or even this month's* outcomes.

That's the power of reimagining business functions—not just improving what we do but transforming *how* we do it for both the external and the internal MEx.

I've had these conversations across industries with marketers and lawyers, accountants and C-suite executives. And what I keep telling them is this: Innovation doesn't always mean inventing the rocket. Sometimes it means asking, Do we even need to launch this rocket? What if we walked there instead? Disruption often comes down to seeing an old problem through a new lens. AI and automation are giving us that new lens. They let us identify bottlenecks. Spot patterns. Surface anomalies. Recommend decisions. And all of that happens fast, accelerating the speed of insight, action, and value creation. But make no mistake—the judgment, the creativity, the context? That still comes from us. The human layer matters more than ever. This is a partnership, not a replacement.

And for organizations that embrace it, the payoff can be extraordinary. According to a 2025 PwC Research report, AI adoption could increase the global economy by up to 15 percent by 2035, a scale comparable to the Industrial Revolution.[3] That's real, tangible value waiting to be unlocked. But only if you're willing to ask the harder questions: What are we still doing today that no longer makes sense? What can we do to delight ME, and why do we think it's true that it would delight them? How often would ME do it, and when would we do it for ME? And most importantly, What could we do tomorrow if we let go of the way we've always done things?

Disruption is coming. You can't always control it. But you can prepare for it. You can shape it. And you can absolutely use it to grow *if* you choose to see it not as a threat but as a launchpad.

The Competitive Edge: AI-Powered Market Intelligence and Decision Velocity

One of the most powerful shifts I've seen with AI and emerging technologies is how they're fundamentally changing the speed and quality of decision-making. And in business, that's everything. I call it decision velocity—not just moving with speed but moving smart and with agility, making small and big changes happen with higher-velocity learning and adjusting based on the feedback loop from MEs.

Let me break it down.

---

3   PwC Research, "AI Adoption Could Boost Global GDP by an Additional 15 Percentage Points by 2035, As Global Economy Is Reshaped," press release, April 29, 2025, https://www.pwc.com/gx/en/news-room/press-releases/2025/ai-adoption-could-boost-global-gdp-by-an-additional-15-percentage.html.

Today's markets move in real time. Customer preferences change overnight. Competitor moves can disrupt your pricing, marketing, and product positioning before you've even scheduled your next leadership offsite. But AI changes the game. It enables leaders to detect market signals the moment they emerge, not after the fact. You can scan for pricing shifts, supply chain bottlenecks, social sentiment, customer churn indicators, and trending demands ... all in the *same* dashboard.

Take competitive intelligence. Imagine you're a major retailer such as Home Depot. You've invested in dynamic, LCD pricing displays across your inventory. With AI monitoring your competitor's online listings, you detect that Lowe's has just dropped the price of a top-selling Milwaukee Sawzall by three dollars. In real time, your system flags the change, and you have a choice: Undercut them by seventy-five cents, match their price, or bundle the product with an attachment to maintain margin and increase perceived value. That's decision velocity. You're not reacting blindly. You're adapting with purpose, guided by insight.

Or consider a boutique fashion brand. Influencer buzz around a certain style or color can change the trajectory of an entire product line in days. With AI-powered social listening and trend analysis, companies can detect rising interest in, say, glittery micro-bags or neon palettes before their competitors. That early awareness informs production, marketing, and even store displays, translating cultural moments into strategic advantage.

Here's another angle. At AWS, I led the team that introduced the free tier, "try before you buy" model that helped explode our adoption. That wasn't a hunch. It came from analyzing usage data across our services. We noticed that once users hit certain thresholds, for volume of storage or number of queries, they were far more likely to expand.

So we asked: How do we lower the barrier to get them there faster? We introduced limited free usage tiers to nudge behavior. It worked. Why? Because it lowered friction, because it was free, because they were less inhibited to try, experiment, and use without fearing to spend a great deal of money to test drive it. Customers discovered value more quickly, became more confident, and committed long-term. But without the patterns from the data, we never would've seen the opportunity. The human insight was critical, but it started with machine-assisted discovery.

This is what makes AI such a force multiplier. It doesn't make the decision for you. It surfaces the signal so you can make the right call faster and with more context.

I see the same pattern across industries. In real estate, predictive analytics can help agents set realistic price expectations by analyzing recent sales, buyer behavior, and market conditions. In manufacturing, digital twins—virtual replicas of physical systems that allow real-time monitoring and simulation—can predict when equipment is about to fail, so maintenance can be proactive, not reactive. In cybersecurity, intelligent monitoring tools can identify suspicious traffic patterns before they become breaches.

And in retail? Imagine a grocery app that notices you've been buying chicken and rice regularly. Now it recommends a Mediterranean dish, preloads your cart with the ingredients, and offers a discount to try something new. Plus, it provides a new healthy recipe for free for ME, who doesn't like variety. What you are doing is saving time for ME, eliminating guesswork, and making it as easy as possible. Personalized, frictionless, and smart. That's not just better service; it's an entirely new layer of competitive edge.

Even more compelling? AI gives smaller players a shot at competing with the giants. It democratizes insight. You don't need a fifty-person analytics team or a seven-figure tech budget. You need the right tools, mindset, and willingness to rethink how decisions get made.

Look at SoFi. Within twelve hours of Ally Bank publicly exiting the mortgage market, SoFi had an email campaign live. For a company to react this quickly while precisely identifying the right potential customers and crafting highly relevant messages requires sophisticated AI infrastructure—the kind that analyzes external market signals, matches them with internal customer data, and personalizes outreach at scale. SoFi's investment in machine learning for risk assessment, conversational AI, and real-time decision-making gives it a competitive edge against larger, more traditional players because it is informed, ready, and equipped to act. That's the new bar.

Speed alone is no longer enough. The combination of speed and relevance—using AI to serve each ME with precision, speed, and relevance that makes every customer feel like the system was built just for them—separates leaders from laggards. It's the ability to see clearly, act decisively, and pivot quickly that creates lasting competitive advantage.

Speed alone is no longer enough. The combination of speed and relevance—using AI to serve each ME with precision, speed, and relevance that makes every customer feel like the system was built just for them—separates leaders from laggards.

Of course, not every insight requires AI. But when you're dealing with massive data volumes, fast-moving variables, and complex ecosystems, the human brain needs help. AI acts like radar. It extends your vision, highlights anomalies, and gives you an early advantage so you can steer more effectively. It's the lever that lets you compete not just today but tomorrow. And the day after that.

The Growth Mindset Shift: Empowering People, Not Replacing Them

There's a lot of hand-wringing about what automation and AI mean for the workforce. And I get it—every time a new wave of technology rolls through, people worry about jobs, about relevance, about being left behind. But I want to reframe the conversation. Because from where I sit, the real opportunity is in freeing people, not replacing them.

This shift starts with mindset. The term *efficiency* has been badly bruised over the years. Say it in the wrong meeting and people immediately brace for cuts. But efficiency doesn't have to mean elimination. In fact, the best use of efficiency is amplification—removing friction so people can focus on the work that actually drives value. Think about it like this. When we transitioned from hunting and gathering to agriculture, the shift freed people to specialize. Some farmed. Others built. Others taught. That leap sparked civilizations. AI and emerging tech are enabling a similar leap, this time in how we work and where we direct human potential.

Or take accounting. I was recently talking with a managing director at a midsize accounting firm. We got into the details of their quarterly P&L process, which took two months and hundreds of hours spent in spreadsheet wrangling, formatting, and manual input. AI and robotic process automation can reduce that to eight minutes. Eight minutes! Now, instead of spending two months looking backward, the team can look forward—analyzing trends, advising clients, and driving strategy. That's not cost-cutting. That's value-creating.

And here's what often gets missed in these conversations: People don't like doing repetitive, low-leverage work. They might tolerate it. But no one dreams of spending their career elbow-deep in macro-laden spreadsheets. What they want is to solve problems, drive growth, and create impact. And automation gives them more space to do just that.

The real challenge is leadership. It's how we talk about these tools. If you frame AI as a way to "do more with less," people hear one thing: layoffs. But if you frame it as "do more of what matters," now you're speaking their language. Now you're giving them a role in the transformation instead of making them fear it. I'll give you a cautionary tale. When Elon Musk took over Twitter, he slashed the workforce by more than half. Twitter still ran, sure—but the ripple effect across the tech industry was profound. Executives elsewhere started asking, "Did we overhire too?" And many responded by initiating cuts of their own, regardless of whether their business warranted it.

Here's the problem: When you cut people reactively, you often lose the very institutional knowledge and customer relationships you need to navigate uncertainty. Then you spend months trying to stabilize the people who remain, months more to retrain and rehire, and by the time the market picks back up, you've lost your momentum … and your trust.

When you cut people reactively, you often lose the very institutional knowledge and customer relationships you need to navigate uncertainty.

There's a better way. Start by identifying the 20 percent of work that consumes 80 percent of your team's time but doesn't move the needle. Automate that. Then take those hours you just reclaimed and redirect them into customer engagement, innovation, and growth.

I've done this with nonprofits, manufacturers, and even internal teams at AWS. In one case, we used AI to streamline the writing of a strategic plan from months of back-and-forth to a four-hour sprint. We freed the team to act on the plan instead of spending months just producing it. That's the difference between efficiency for cost and efficiency for capacity.

This is the heart of what I call a growth mindset in digital transformation: using technology not just to get lean but to get better. Not to shrink your workforce but to multiply its impact. Here's where the culture piece comes in. When your team sees that automation is being used to support them, not replace them, they lean in. They look for improvements. They help identify what to streamline next. They become coarchitects of transformation, not victims of it.

That's where momentum comes from. That's how you start to build a truly adaptive organization.

You can test this approach immediately: Pick one broken handoff this week, bring the involved parties together for 90 minutes, and map what seamless would look like. That's how transformation starts—one conversation at a time.

Whether you're leading a team or an entire organization, start with this: Identify the tedious, the repetitive, the low-leverage. Then ask: What could my team do if we didn't have to do that anymore? And what systems, tools, and training would it need to make that next leap? Because when you stop looking at efficiency as subtraction and start seeing it as expansion, that's when real transformation begins.

Your Mission Possible—from Paralysis to Action

I've been in more executive meetings than I can count where someone eventually leans back, exhales, and says, "OK, but where do we start?" And I get it. When you're facing down digital transformation, especially with the speed and scope of change we're experiencing now, it can feel like staring up at a mountain from the bottom. You know you need to climb, but the first step isn't obvious, and the weight of uncertainty can keep you frozen in place.

That's where so many transformations stall before they begin. Not because people don't care. Not because the opportunity isn't real. But because *there's no blueprint.* No clear architecture from vision to execution. And that lack of clarity creates hesitation, which, in a fast-moving environment, is a risk all its own. This book is your blueprint. It's your playbook to shift from overwhelm to opportunity; from asking, What if? to declaring, Why not us? Because the truth is, you don't have to have it all figured out to begin with. You just need to start asking the right questions and have a framework to help identify the right steps for your organization to move forward. What are the frictions that frustrate your customers? What repetitive tasks bog down your employees? Where do delays pile up and decisions get stuck? What could be simpler, smarter, and faster if only you had the right tools, right mindset, and right support?

To help you get started on this journey, I've created the Digital Capability Assessment that you can access through the following QR code. This assessment will help you unpack these early questions and provide clarity about where you stand today so you can build your future more intentionally. You'll find this QR code throughout the book, which will take you to the Insights Hub—an exclusive corner of my website, accessible only to readers of *Everybody Wins*.

This is where your *mission possible* begins.

I use that phrase deliberately—mission possible—because too often the conversation around transformation feels like science fiction. Jetpacks. Robots. Sci-fi-level change. But in reality, successful transformation doesn't come from moonshots. It comes from identifying new business models and processes, and new ways to operate too. These core principles are often way more important than the shiny new thing.

Let me give you an example. I worked with a traditional print media company that had long relied on events for revenue. When the pandemic hit, those events disappeared. But even when gathering places reopened, they clung to the same playbook: "Let's get back to what we used to do." The problem was that the audience had changed. The engagement model had changed. So we helped them rethink everything: how to personalize content recommendations, how to build recurring digital engagement, how to turn data into insights that could power better events and better experiences between events. They didn't stop being a media company, but they did become a smarter, more adaptive one. That's a mission possible.

Another example? Higher education. The traditional model of one-size-fits-all classroom learning is under pressure from rising costs, digital-native students, and employers demanding different outcomes. But instead of fighting the shift, some institutions are embracing hybrid delivery models, immersive learning platforms, and intelligent learning analytics that help students stay on track. They're using emerging technologies not to replace educators but to support better outcomes. That's transformation with purpose.

Every industry has its version of this. Energy companies navigating renewables. Banks rethinking customer experience. Manufacturers investing in predictive maintenance and digital twins. It's happening everywhere. The question isn't if disruption is coming but whether you're willing to shape it before it shapes you. And here's the kicker: Your competitors—especially digital-native ones—aren't waiting. They're not encumbered by legacy systems or "we've always done it this way" thinking. They're agile by design. They're structured for speed. And if you're standing still, they're gaining ground, whether you see it or not.

But you're not stuck. That's the message I want you to take from this chapter. You can absolutely compete. You can absolutely lead. And you don't need to be a technical leader to win. Many execs say, "this is my CIO/CTO's problem," because of internal politics or lack of understanding. The fact is, it's *everyone's* issue. You need to be a company that uses technology intelligently, to enhance customer experience through business models and all touchpoints on the customer journey that optimize for MEx.

Will there be resistance? Of course. People fear what they don't understand. That's human. People innately fear what change means to them without regard for customers or the business because they fear loss of control and can't see how the change benefits all. Yet fear is rarely the biggest obstacle. It's inertia. It's the comfort with what's familiar. And that's why leadership matters. Because real transformation doesn't start in the IT department. It starts in the C-suite. In fact, it starts with *you*.

So here's what I want to leave you with: You're not behind. You're at the beginning. And the fact that you're holding this book tells me something important—you're ready. Ready to look differently at what's possible. Ready to lead with clarity and courage. Ready to build a future that serves your customers, your employees, and your business in ways you might not have thought possible until now.

In the chapters ahead, I'll walk you through the frameworks, the use cases, and the mindsets that make digital transformation actionable. You'll learn how to assess your readiness, prioritize your efforts, and lead change at a pace your organization can absorb and sustain. We'll start small. We'll build smart. And we'll focus relentlessly on value—because that's how lasting transformation happens. You don't need to jump in all at once, but you do need to jump, because the burning platform is real, and what's waiting on the other side isn't fear. It's growth and a future built on possibility, powered by your leadership. Remember that oil rig worker who leapt into the North Sea to escape the horrific fire? He lived to tell the story!

FIVE STEPS TO TAKE NOW

I've said it before, and I'll say it again: The biggest blocker to transformation isn't fear—it's inertia. It's the pressure of the urgent crowding out the important. The goal of this section is to help you *break that inertia*—not with theory but with specific, tactical steps you can start taking right now.

You don't need to overhaul your organization overnight. But you do need to begin. So here are five practical steps—grounded in my experience working with companies, governments, and universities around the world—to help you build momentum in your digital transformation journey.

Step 1: Take the AI Business Stress Test

AI is one of the most important enablers of modern transformation, but many organizations still don't know where they stand. Scan the QR code to take your own AI Business Stress Test. This assessment will help you gauge your organization's AI readiness. Answer honestly—this is about clarity, not judgment.

Step 2: Identify Your "Burning Platform"

What's the metaphorical fire beneath your feet?

It could be, for example:

- Slowing customer engagement
- Stagnant growth
- Process inefficiency
- Losing talent to more tech-savvy competitors
- Inability to respond quickly to market shifts
- Declining margins in a previously profitable area

Spend fifteen minutes with your leadership team this week and ask:

What are the business conditions that would make staying where we are more dangerous than moving forward?

This is about urgency—but rooted in *opportunity*, not panic. If you don't identify the fire, you'll never find the courage to jump.

Step 3: Map One Friction Point

Pick one part of your customer journey, employee workflow, or internal process that you *know* is frustrating. Then ask:

- What's the goal here?
- What slows it down?
- What could be automated?
- Where is human creativity or judgment needed?
- What would success look like if this were optimized?

You don't need AI to answer these questions. But asking them starts the process of rethinking how you create and deliver value. This is where innovation begins—on the ground, with real problems and a lens of curiosity.

Step 4: Host a "Mission Possible" Workshop

Bring together five to eight cross-functional leaders or team members for sixty minutes.

Agenda:

1. Define what transformation means for your organization.
2. Brainstorm three to five areas where digital tools could improve outcomes.
3. Pick one initiative and write your "mission possible" statement:

"What if we could [desired outcome] by [new approach] using [tool or capability]?"

Example:
"What if we could reduce customer onboarding time from two weeks to two days by using digital document processing and an AI-powered walkthrough?"

Keep it aspirational *and* achievable. Use this as a North Star to begin experimentation.

Step 5: Reframe Efficiency as Empowerment

If you take away one thing from this chapter, let it be this:

Automation isn't about doing more with less—it's about doing *more of what matters*.

Start shifting the conversation inside your organization:

- From cutting costs → to creating new and improved capabilities
- From reducing headcount → to reimagining roles
- From productivity metrics → to value creation metrics

Identify one process that's sucking up valuable human time on your team—and commit to exploring ways to automate or simplify it. Then redeploy that time toward customer engagement, innovation, or strategic growth.

People need to *see* that efficiency doesn't mean elimination. It means elevation.

Final Thought: Transformation Starts with You

Don't wait for the perfect strategy. Start with a bias for action. I've seen organizations stuck for years in planning loops—waiting for "more data," "better timing," or "executive alignment." But the ones that break through don't wait for perfect—they act, they learn, and they adapt. Very good edging in on great beats perfect every time.

Start small. Start focused. But start now. You have the tools. You have the insights. And you have a partner in this book to walk you through the rest.

MISSION
POSSIBLE

CHAPTER TWO

CHARTING YOUR COURSE

Defining Your Digital Vision and Strategy

The essence of strategy is choosing what not to do.
—MICHAEL PORTER

Your Mission Possible Blueprint: Strategy without execution is just planning theater. In this chapter, we'll discuss how to move from vision to action with clarity and confidence. You'll finish with a framework for defining your digital North Star and five practical steps to start building momentum immediately.

WHEN I FIRST walked into a strategic planning session with the US Space Force Association, it was clear they were facing a familiar challenge: too many voices, too many priorities, too little time. They were growing at a rapid pace, and that growth had brought with it a tidal wave of demands from industry, academia, and across the defense ecosystem. The instinct among their leadership team was to handle things the traditional way. That essentially meant drafting a long, detailed plan over the course of weeks or months, involving a committee, passing revisions around, and eventually ending up with a document that might check the boxes but likely wouldn't inspire action or clarity. This was the playbook they knew.

But I could immediately see that the real problem wasn't time, it was *focus*. What they needed went beyond a plan. They needed strategic clarity, delivered with speed and done in a way that didn't bog down the very people they needed to lead the charge.

So I asked one question: "What are we really trying to do here?"

That question flipped the script. Instead of talking tactics or drafting templates, we started with goals. Who were they trying to help? What were the outcomes those groups cared about? Why would those outcomes matter, and how would success be measured? These questions were the anchors of the strategy. And they gave us permission to rethink the entire process.

So I set up a video meeting with the Space Force Association leader and leveraged intelligent transcription capabilities. The conversation was structured exactly how you'd read a strategic plan. We talked through each goal, the reasons it mattered, the people it would benefit, and the ways success could be tracked. Nothing was written down manually, and no one was scrambling to take notes. The automated system captured it all.

After the call, I exported the transcript, cleaned it up, and organized it by theme. Then I used a generative AI model to translate those sections into an executive narrative format that was tight, digestible, and actionable. The AI captured tone, structure, and relevance, tailored for a senior audience that didn't have time to wade through twenty pages of corporate jargon.

In less than two hours, we had a working draft of a five-goal strategic plan, complete with an executive summary, key decisions for review, and even a compelling cover image generated by an AI design tool. What normally would've taken weeks of staff time and multiple cycles of review was produced in a single afternoon.

If you're already leveraging similar tools and processes in your own workflows, then you know just how much time and effort AI technologies can save you. Even in its most rudimentary forms, AI enables our human capacity. As the technology continues to evolve, so too will our ability to focus on what truly matters.

The real breakthrough with the Space Force Association's strategic plan, however, wasn't the speed. It was the shift in thinking. By using AI to handle the mindless details, we were able to be more mindful about our mission, our members, and the future of our organization.

Instead of defaulting to, How are we going to do this? we asked, What are we trying to achieve, and for whom? That distinction made all the difference. It allowed us to move smartly, not just quickly. We built a strategic tool that catalyzed alignment and decision-making.

This kind of approach isn't just for military organizations or fast-moving startups. It's for any leader willing to rethink how strategy gets done. Whether you're in healthcare, manufacturing, financial services, or retail, the principles remain the same. Start with the outcome that matters to your stakeholders. Use AI and digital tools to capture and organize thinking quickly. Then iterate based on real feedback, not theoretical planning cycles. Too often, leaders jump into execution mode. They fire off initiatives, select tools, and spin up projects without clearly defining the destination. It's fire, ready, aim. And then they wonder why they missed the target.

What the Space Force Association planning session reminded me is this: When you start with the right questions, you get better answers. You uncover what actually matters, and you empower your team not with more work but with more clarity. The real value is getting the ideas and knowledge out of people's minds and into actionable documents as quickly and efficiently as possible, letting technology handle the writing and formatting. It's like starting in the red zone in football versus driving the full length of the field from your own one-yard line. And when you apply AI and digital tools with a purpose, you unlock efficiency and transformation.

When you start with the right questions,
you get better answers.

That's what charting your course is really about: stepping back to get clear on where you're going, why you're going there, and who you're bringing along for the journey.

Digital Vision Begins with Purpose, Not Tools

Most executives are wired to solve problems. You give them a challenge, and they're off to the races assembling teams, selecting tools, and building solutions. This trait makes them decisive, but it also puts them in that "fire-ready-aim" mindset, not fully understanding the what, who, or why before jumping to how.

This is not surprising when you think about it. Most leadership environments reward action. You get asked to launch something, fix something, or improve something, and the natural impulse is to get it done. But moving fast in the wrong direction gets you lost, only faster.

When I coach executives through digital transformation, the first thing I ask them to do is *pause*—not indefinitely, but long enough to gain strategic clarity. I call it a "strategic pause," a deliberate break from the rush of execution to answer foundational questions: Who are we trying to serve? What does success look like for them? Why does it matter? When do they need it?

Without this foundation, any digital strategy, AI-driven or otherwise, risks being a house built on sand. Take AI, for example. It's the buzzword on every boardroom agenda. But too many leaders talk about AI in isolation. They want to do something with AI without first clarifying what problem they're solving or what outcome they're driving toward. That's like packing your suitcase before you've chosen a vacation destination. The result is often wasted effort and misalignment that create more confusion than clarity.

A good digital vision starts with purpose. It begins with understanding who your customers are, what your employees need to succeed, and how your business creates value. It asks the hard questions early to ensure the work that follows actually matters.

A good digital vision starts with purpose.

Here's where the digital vision becomes more than a PowerPoint slide or a talking point at a leadership retreat. When defined well, it becomes a compass. It guides decisions about where to invest, what to build, what to automate, and what to leave behind. It also gives employees a sense of meaning. People don't get inspired by tools; they get inspired by purpose. If they can see how their work contributes to a meaningful outcome, they're far more likely to engage and deliver at a higher level.

I often remind executives that their digital strategy isn't simply about adding technology. It's about reshaping their business to compete and grow in a new reality. That kind of change requires intent and purpose. And purpose is what turns tech from a cost center into a value driver.

Think about your organization. Are your teams aligned around a shared outcome or are they busy executing disconnected tasks? Do your AI initiatives serve clearly defined business goals or are they experiments in search of purpose? These are tough questions, but they're the right ones to ask.

One of the most powerful things a leader can do is take that pause and think with precision. To define the vision, not just assume it. Because once that clarity is in place, the how becomes a whole lot easier to get right.

Avoiding AI-Washing

We're living in an era where AI is the headline of nearly every business pitch, investor deck, and marketing campaign. That's a problem. The term *AI-washing* has entered the business lexicon for a reason. It describes the growing trend of companies slapping the AI label onto products or services without meaningful integration or customer benefit. It's become a shortcut to signal innovation, regardless of whether any true innovation has occurred.

But here's the thing: Customers and stakeholders are getting smarter. They can spot the difference between a company that's thoughtfully applying AI to solve real problems and one that's simply using it as window dressing.

I saw this firsthand with a SaaS customer relationship management (CRM) vendor that had bolted a chatbot onto its customer support interface. On paper, it was labeled "AI-enabled customer service." In practice, it was a frustrating experience. The chatbot lacked context, couldn't handle basic queries, and ended up escalating issues back to human agents, adding friction instead of removing it.

The result? Customers began questioning the credibility of the company's entire digital strategy. The technology didn't fail because AI was the wrong tool; it failed because it was implemented without a clear understanding of the customer journey. It was AI for the sake of AI.

This is the essence of AI-washing: talking about technology without connecting it to outcomes. Leaders fall into this trap when they feel pressure to keep up with the competition, to be seen as forward-thinking, or to satisfy investors who are chasing the next big thing. But the danger is real. When customers encounter AI experiences that are clunky, confusing, or irrelevant, they don't blame the implementation; they blame the brand. And once that trust erodes, it's hard to win back.

Authentic AI strategy starts with value. What are you trying to solve? Who benefits from the solution? How does AI make the experience better, faster, simpler, and/or more reliable? If you can't answer those questions, you shouldn't be launching the initiative. In reality, the best AI applications are invisible. They enhance the customer experience without drawing attention to themselves. They anticipate needs, personalize responses, simplify decisions, and help people get what they want with less friction. That's where trust is built.

Authentic AI strategy starts with value.

It's also worth remembering that AI is not a magic wand. It's a tool that requires clean, well-structured data. It needs thoughtful design, and it works best when it's aligned to a clearly defined outcome. That alignment is what separates genuine innovation from digital theater.

Leaders have a responsibility here. It's not enough to delegate AI initiatives to the IT department or slap an AI label on a product feature and call it done. You have to own the vision and ensure the work being done connects to your business goals, your customer needs, and your brand promise.

There's nothing wrong with experimenting, as innovation often starts with trial and error. But experimentation still needs a strategy. If you're launching an AI-driven chatbot, for example, don't just ask what it can do. Ask how it makes life easier for your customers. Ask what success looks like and how you'll measure it. In a world saturated with AI buzzwords, the companies that will win are those that move beyond the hype to align their digital strategy with customer outcomes.

Customer-Centric Visioning: The North Star Approach

If there's one principle that should guide every digital transformation effort, it's this: Start with the customer and work backward. Too many strategies begin with internal capabilities or competitive pressures. But true digital maturity means designing your approach from the perspective of the people you're trying to serve. This mindset shift, from inside out to outside in, is where transformation gets real.

Let's take a moment to look at the digital customer journey beyond just a series of transactions. It's a complete experience that begins before a customer ever clicks a button or talks to a representative, and it includes every step, from initial awareness and consideration to purchase, support, retention, and advocacy. Each of these touchpoints is an opportunity to earn trust ... or lose it.

DIGITAL CUSTOMER JOURNEY

AWARENESS

Mindset: The customer doesn't know they need you yet. Your job is to listen for their pain points and to be where they're looking. This isn't about broadcasting; it's about being discovered at the precise moment you're most relevant.

AI Opportunity: Predictive analytics can identify potential customer segments and target them with personalized, relevant content before they even search for you, transforming passive marketing into proactive value delivery.

CONSIDERATION

Mindset: The customer knows they have a problem and is evaluating solutions. Don't sell them; help them make a confident decision. This is about making their research phase simple and their choice clear.

AI Opportunity: A smart AI assistant or chatbot can answer their specific questions in real-time and provide them with personalized case studies, testimonials, or pricing that is tailored to their needs. This makes the evaluation feel less like a sales pitch and more like a helpful consultation.

PURCHASE

Mindset: The moment of truth. Every step here needs to be frictionless, fast, and secure. Any confusion or delay is an opportunity for them to walk away. The MEx philosophy demands a purchase process that is effortless, not just easy.

AI Opportunity: An AI-driven checkout flow can auto-fill forms, offer personalized payment options, or suggest a bundle based on their preferences, making the process effortless and fast. This not only increases conversion but also reinforces the feeling that you know and value their time.

SUPPORT & RETENTION

Mindset: The sale is not the end of the journey; it's the beginning of the relationship. Anticipate their needs and provide them with proactive support that goes beyond a reactive help desk.

AI Opportunity: An AI system can detect potential issues before they become a problem, providing them with a self-service solution or automatically routing them to the right human for help. This transforms support from a cost center into a powerful tool for building loyalty.

ADVOCACY

Mindset: The customer is no longer just a customer—they're your best marketing asset. Empower them to share their positive experience and become a force multiplier for your brand.

AI Opportunity: AI can identify your most engaged and satisfied customers and prompt them to write a review or refer a friend at the optimal time and in the most frictionless way. This turns a passive customer into an active advocate.

A customer-centric digital strategy starts by deeply understanding these moments. What are your customers trying to do at each stage? Where do they encounter friction? What matters most to them? How do they define a good experience?

One client I worked with wanted to create a new customer self-service portal. They had thousands of technical manuals scattered across different systems, and customers often called support just to locate basic information. The first instinct from the team was to create a knowledge base app and populate it with links. But we paused and asked a more foundational question: What did their customers really want?

Well, they wanted to find an answer quickly. They didn't want to scroll through PDFs or guess at keyword searches. They wanted a single, reliable, frictionless experience that delivered the right information immediately. That insight changed everything for the client. Instead of building an app that mirrored internal complexity, we designed a guided, intuitive experience that anticipated user needs and delivered precise results. The feedback was immediate: reduced support calls and measurable gains in loyalty.

That's the power of working backward. It helps you see the whole picture and align every touchpoint to serve a coherent experience.

This approach also demands that we treat every customer interaction as part of a larger relationship, not just a one-off transaction. For digital visioning to be customer-centric, it must consider what makes the experience lovable, not just functional. That's why I often encourage organizations to focus on the minimal lovable product rather than the minimal viable product. Viable might get you through the door, but lovable makes people want to come back.

That's the power of working backward. It helps you see the whole picture and align every touchpoint to serve a coherent experience.

This same thinking applies to employees as well. A digital vision rooted in customer needs but disconnected from internal workflows will fall flat. You have to ask: Are we making our employees' lives easier so they can better serve the customer? Is the system intuitive? Does it eliminate manual work? Are we delivering mission speed and agility? Or are we just adding new layers of complexity?

This is why customer-centric visioning must be viewed not as a marketing exercise but as a strategic imperative. It forces alignment and requires cross-functional collaboration. And it surfaces trade-offs that must be consciously made, which may mean simplifying processes, sunsetting legacy systems, or investing in data infrastructure to provide a unified view of the customer.

And speaking of data, this is where digital visioning meets AI. Because once you've defined what the customer experience should look like, AI becomes a powerful enabler. It can help personalize the journey, anticipate needs, and resolve issues before they escalate. But none of that matters if you don't have clean, connected, high-quality data. AI can't solve for a lack of clarity; it can only amplify what's already there.

So what's your North Star? Is it customer effort reduction? Personalization at scale? Seamless omnichannel support? Whatever it is, define it clearly and let it shape your priorities. Then work backward to design every process, every interaction, and every tool to serve that vision.

Diagnosing Digital Maturity

One of the most critical steps in any transformation effort is knowing where you stand before deciding where to go. Without that clarity, you're essentially launching a mission without a map. Diagnosing digital maturity is how you avoid that mistake. It's your compass. It tells you whether you're ready to scale, where your gaps are, and what kind of help you might need.

Digitally mature organizations consistently outperform their peers in two key areas: revenue growth and cost efficiency. While less mature companies tend to focus on using digital tools simply to cut costs, digitally mature companies take it a step further. They see technology as a way to unlock new revenue streams and opportunities that were never possible before.

Consider the analogy of two different companies building a wall. The first company's leader focused only on buying cheaper bricks and paying the workers less. They built the same wall, just for a little less money. But the second company's leader used a machine to create the bricks on-site, a drone to fly them to the top, and a digital model to show the workers exactly where each one went. In the end, company two not only saved money and time in comparison to the first company, but they also built a stronger, more beautiful, and completely custom wall.

That's the kind of distinction we're talking about. In my experience, digitally mature companies optimize existing processes to reinvent the business itself. They have no interest in doing things the old way or the supposedly cheaper way. For these organizations, it's about doing entirely new things that create massive value for customers.

But let's be clear: Digital maturity isn't measured by technical capabilities or a checklist of systems and software. It's a reflection of your organization's mindset, culture, processes, and willingness to evolve. This mindset, backed by the right data and technology, is what separates market leaders from everyone else.

I often begin these conversations with a few simple but powerful questions: How open is your organization to rethinking how it works? Are you willing to challenge "the way we've always done it"? Can your teams collaborate across functions to deliver a unified experience? Are you leveraging data in real time to guide decision-making? Do you know where your data lives? And is that data accessible, clean, and actionable?

These questions don't require a PhD in computer science, but they do require honesty.

Some of the most resistant organizations I've encountered weren't lacking in budget or technology. They were lacking in mindset and were too attached to legacy processes, siloed structures, and a belief that what worked yesterday will work tomorrow. They were protecting what they knew instead of preparing for what's next. The truth is, if you're not willing to change how you work, no technology will save you.

THE DIGITALLY MATURE MINDSET

At the end of the day, digital maturity is about readiness. Are you ready to reengineer how your business creates and delivers value? Are you ready to build systems that evolve with your customers instead of reacting to them? Are you ready to empower employees with the tools and insights they need to be faster, smarter, and more agile?

This brand of readiness needs to be embedded in the company culture. When I ask executives how digitally mature their organization is, they'll sometimes talk about their AI pilots or cloud migration. That's great, but then I ask how many frontline employees understand the company's digital goals. That's usually met with silence.

If your people don't know where you're going or why it matters, you haven't achieved digital maturity; you've just upgraded your tech stack.

DIGITAL MATURITY AND SCOPE

Assessing maturity also means being clear about scope. Not everything needs to be transformed at once. But the areas that are in focus should be treated with discipline and depth. Too many leaders scatter their energy across too many initiatives, each one underfunded and under-resourced. That's a recipe for fatigue and failure. Maturity means knowing what not to pursue just as much as knowing what to prioritize.

DIGITAL MATURITY AND YOUR DATA

Another lens I encourage leaders to use is data. Your data ecosystem is a mirror of your digital maturity. Is it centralized or fragmented? Is it governed or chaotic? Can it be used to power AI-driven insights, or is it trapped in spreadsheets and disconnected systems? Try as you might, you can't fake data readiness. AI doesn't compensate for bad data; it actually magnifies it. So if your systems can't talk to each other, if your analytics are lagging, or if your teams are constantly firefighting to find answers, that's a signal you're not where you need to be. The good news is that these are solvable problems. But you have to acknowledge them first.

THE HUMAN SIDE OF DIGITAL MATURITY

There's also a human side to maturity. How do your teams respond to change? Are they empowered to experiment and learn? Or are they stuck in fear-based compliance, afraid to try something new in case it fails? Do your leaders model digital curiosity, or do they delegate it to others?

The main question here is whether the organization is actually structured to reward new ideas, new ways of working. Having an "attempt and fail and try again" culture is critical. You cannot assume what you try will work the first time and deliver immediate quantifiable value. Sometimes, the largest initial value is trying, and if you fail, try again.

Your digital maturity reflects the maturity of your leadership. If your mindset is fixed, your strategy will be brittle. But if your mindset is adaptive and you see transformation as an ongoing evolution, not a onetime project, you'll be positioned to lead.

Strategy in Motion

A strong digital vision cannot remain isolated from how a business operates. To lead real transformation, that vision must shape execution across the organization in ways that are both intentional and measurable. Strategy should not exist as a high-level document disconnected from the reality of daily operations. Instead, it needs to be lived through systems, processes, and behaviors that reflect its direction.

A strong digital vision cannot remain isolated from how a business operates.

With the increasing impact of AI, this becomes even more critical. The most effective digital strategies aren't static plans but living frameworks that evolve as you learn. You're ultimately responsible for executing your strategy, but AI enables you to continuously level up that execution by surfacing patterns, predicting outcomes, and revealing new opportunities as market conditions shift.

Operational agility becomes the key in this. The organizations that succeed are the ones that design with speed and flexibility in mind. Their leaders know how to turn strategy into movement by eliminating friction points in execution, anticipating customer and employee pain, and using data to intervene before problems become visible.

In working with a regional grocery chain, I saw firsthand what this looks like in practice. Their leadership had solid objectives, but they struggled to translate those goals into improved customer experience. Products were frequently out of stock, staffing didn't match traffic patterns, and the stores weren't delivering on the promise of convenience. We reframed their digital strategy to focus on operational responsiveness. By applying AI to forecast demand at the store level, we gave managers the insight to plan smarter, reduce inventory waste, and adjust layouts based on real customer flow.

This approach works because it moves from broad vision to targeted action. Instead of reacting to symptoms, it addresses the root causes of inefficiency. Friction often stems from decisions made without visibility or coordination. Digital tools can solve for that, but only when leaders have the discipline to connect those tools to clear business priorities.

The thing is, every digital initiative must be anchored in a specific business goal. Whether the objective is to increase revenue, reduce churn, improve efficiency, or enable growth, the connection between purpose and project must be explicit. Too often, organizations chase technology trends without asking whether the outcome supports the broader strategy. The result is a pile of fragmented efforts that deliver activity but not impact.

Every digital initiative must be anchored in a specific business goal.

In one case, I worked with a large manufacturer that had poured resources into digital tools aimed at improving internal workflows. On the surface, it seemed like a step forward. But when we stepped back, it became clear the investments had been made with no alignment to customer value. The company had digitized complexity instead of simplifying outcomes. We asked harder questions: What are your customers actually trying to achieve? What do they expect from their experience with you? How do your digital tools support that? The answers revealed a need to shift focus from internal optimization to customer-facing innovation.

That shift required rethinking more than process. It required reimagining how the business model could serve as a connected, tech-enabled journey rather than a set of siloed departments. Digital transformation should challenge the organization to see its services as experiences. That perspective makes it easier to identify where change will matter most and where automation or AI can create real leverage.

But identifying opportunities is not enough. Success comes from measuring progress against the right indicators. Key performance indicators (KPIs) are the compass points of a digital strategy. When well chosen, these metrics help teams adjust course, make better decisions, and maintain alignment across functions. But to truly support AI-driven transformation, many traditional operational metrics need to be restructured. In a world where strategic initiatives often cut across departments, success can no longer be measured solely through siloed, functional KPIs. Organizations must design cross-functional success measures that reflect shared ownership and collective outcomes. For example, if the strategic objective is to grow market share in a specific segment—requiring coordinated shifts in pricing, promotions, and fulfillment—then the resulting increase in inventory or transportation costs should still be recognized as a win for both the sales/marketing and supply chain teams. Without rethinking how success is defined and rewarded across functions, organizations risk undermining the very innovation they're aiming to drive.

Metrics That Matter in the Age of MEx

In a digital era when customers expect personalized experiences and individual attention, creating more reports is easy; the real challenge is using data to drive better decisions that genuinely enhance each customer's experience. As business leaders, data analysts, marketers, and customer experience managers, your role in this is crucial. The metrics that truly matter show tangible business value, not just activity.

Here are the most critical types of KPIs to track for your digital transformation in the age of MEx:

1. CUSTOMER EXPERIENCE AND LOYALTY (THE MEx THERMOMETER)

These KPIs directly measure how well you meet customer expectations and build lasting relationships. By tracking these, you'll know if your efforts truly delight each ME customer.

- **Net promoter score (NPS):** Are customers so delighted by personalized experiences that they'll recommend you? This gauges their overall loyalty.

- **Customer satisfaction score:** How satisfied are customers with specific interactions, especially those enhanced by data or AI? This tells you if your tailored approaches are hitting the mark.

- **Customer effort score:** How easy can a customer get what they need across any channel? Lower effort means a more frictionless, personalized experience.

- **Customer churn rate:** Are your personalized efforts effectively reducing the number of customers leaving?

- **Customer lifetime value:** Are tailored offerings and proactive engagement leading to customers spending more with you over their entire relationship? This is the ultimate measure of MEx value.

2. ENGAGEMENT AND PERSONALIZATION EFFECTIVENESS

These metrics show how well your personalized efforts resonate and drive desired actions. They reveal whether your tailored content and features truly capture each individual customer's attention and drive their engagement.

- **Personalized conversion rate:** What percentage of individuals complete a desired action (such as a purchase or sign-up) when presented with a specifically tailored offer or recommendation?

- **Personalized feature adoption rate:** For new digital features designed for unique needs, how many users are actively engaging with them?

- **Engagement rate (per user/session):** How much time are individuals spending interacting with your personalized content or digital touchpoints? This shows if your tailored experiences are sticky.

- **Return visit frequency:** Are customers returning more often because the experience is consistently personalized and valuable to them?

3. OPERATIONAL EFFICIENCY (ENABLING MEx AT SCALE)

These KPIs ensure you deliver individual value efficiently, without breaking the bank. They help guarantee a seamless experience for *every* ME customer, even at high volumes.

- **First-contact resolution rate:** How often are individual customer issues entirely resolved on the first interaction, ideally through personalized self-service (such as a chatbot that can address specific customer queries) or highly informed agents (who have access to a customer's entire interaction history and can provide personalized solutions)? This indicates truly frictionless service.

- **Average resolution time for personalized inquiries:** How quickly are unique, tailored customer issues being resolved? Faster resolution means a better experience for the ME customer.

- **Cost per engaged customer:** Are you efficiently acquiring and retaining customers through personalized strategies? This indicator measures the cost-effectiveness of your MEx-focused efforts.

4. FINANCIAL IMPACT

Ultimately, these metrics show how your age of MEx strategies affect your bottom line. These are the numbers that directly link your personalization efforts to your company's overall growth and profitability. The potential impact is significant, and the urgency to act is clear.

- **Revenue from personalized channels/offers:** What percentage of your revenue comes directly from campaigns or recommendations tailored to individuals?
- **Return on personalization investment:** What's the direct financial return on investment (ROI) for your efforts to personalize customer experiences? This proves the business case for your digital transformation.

These metrics directly connect to your bottom line and strategic goals, showing that data isn't just about more information but about smarter action and superior, individualized customer experiences in the age of MEx.

As such, the metrics that matter must always reflect value. These are the signals that tell you whether your strategy is moving the business in the right direction, regardless of whether you're just getting started with data-driven decision-making or already have sophisticated analytics in place.

It is tempting to reach for what's easy to measure. But digital maturity requires leaders to prioritize what matters over what's convenient. That means resisting vanity metrics and selecting indicators that foster transparency, learning, and course correction. The right KPIs do much more than monitor progress; they shape behavior.

The right KPIs do much more than monitor progress;
they shape behavior.

When digital vision informs operational strategy and aligns tightly with business goals, the impact is visible. Teams move faster with more clarity, while customers receive more personalized, consistent experiences. In turn, leaders gain the confidence that their investments are delivering meaningful value. Done properly, this is how digital transformation becomes embedded in the way the business thinks and scales.

FIVE STEPS TO TAKE NOW

Defining a digital strategy shouldn't feel like navigating a fog. But for many organizations, the process starts with too many ideas and no clear sense of where they all lead. The goal of this section is to help you move from reactive execution to purposeful strategy, using tools and mindsets grounded in my real-world work with organizations of every size and sector.

Start small. Start clear. Start with purpose. These five steps will help you build momentum.

Step 1: Take a Strategic Pause

Before you initiate another tool rollout or approve the next AI pilot, step back. Schedule a one-hour strategic pause with your core leadership team. Ask and answer four foundational questions:

- Who are we trying to serve?
- What outcome matters most to them?
- Why does that outcome matter now?
- How will we know we've succeeded?

Document the answers. This is much more than a brainstorming session; it's actually the beginning of alignment. If you can't articulate the purpose of a digital initiative in a single sentence, it's not ready for execution.

Step 2: Audit for AI-Washing

Take stock of your current and planned AI initiatives. For each one, ask these questions:

- What problem is this solving?
- Who benefits from the solution?
- How does this application improve the UX?

If you can't clearly connect the technology to a business outcome, reconsider or refine the initiative. AI is the tool that *enables* the strategy, not a strategy in and of itself. This audit helps you avoid the costly trap of digital theater.

Step 3: Define Your North Star Customer Experience

Gather a cross-functional group, and walk through a single customer journey from start to finish—awareness, purchase, onboarding, support, retention. Ask:

- Where do customers encounter friction?
- What would a seamless experience look like at each step?
- How would AI or automation enhance, not complicate, that journey?

Then, write a North Star statement: "We want our customers to experience [X] in a way that is [Y]." Let this be the lens through which you evaluate every digital decision moving forward.

Step 4: Launch a Digital Maturity Conversation

Host a leadership meeting with one agenda item: assessing your digital maturity. Frame the conversation with simple but powerful prompts:

- How easily can we act on our data?
- Are our teams aligned around shared outcomes or siloed in tasks?
- How adaptable are our systems when priorities shift?

Resist the urge to quantify too soon. This is about surfacing blind spots and catalyzing a shared understanding of where transformation needs to focus. What emerges here becomes the blueprint for targeted growth.

Step 5: Build a Value-Driven Strategy Sprint

Set aside two hours with a transformation task force to build a draft strategy sprint. Structure it around outcomes:

- Select one business goal (e.g., reduce customer churn by 15 percent).
- Identify one customer or employee pain point impacting that goal.
- Design a thirty-day pilot that leverages digital tools to address the pain point.
- Define what success looks like and how you'll measure it.

This is how you move from static strategy documents to living, adaptive strategy in motion. It shows your teams what progress looks like without the burden of perfectionism.

PART II

LEADING THE CHARGE

CHAPTER THREE

BREAKING DOWN SILOS

Fostering Collaboration and Agility

If you want to go fast, go alone. If you want to go far, go together.
—AFRICAN PROVERB

Your Mission Possible Blueprint: Collaboration isn't optional in the age of AI—it's competitive advantage. This chapter shows you how to break down the barriers that slow transformation and build the teamwork that accelerates it. You'll finish with five specific actions to improve cross-functional effectiveness immediately.

I WORKED WITH a cybersecurity startup not long ago that was facing a challenge common among fast-growing companies. Its product had gained traction and its client list was growing. But it was operating in a way that limited its ability to scale, and that was starting to hurt the business.

The startup's approach was rooted in customization where every client engagement included deep, personalized support. Engineers tailored each implementation while customer success teams worked closely with every new user. This earned them loyalty early on, but as they grew, the model created tension. Each new client added more complexity, and the teams were maxed out. Engineering fell behind. Sales had to choose between bringing in new business and maintaining existing relationships. And the internal conflict was increasing. The systems weren't broken, but they weren't built for the next stage either.

I could see clearly that the teams were misaligned because they lacked a shared view of the outcome they were trying to achieve. Engineering optimized for stability, sales pushed for speed, and customer support tried to maintain satisfaction. But there was no common thread tying it all together.

That's when I suggested a different path. We built a transformation team that looked less like a typical project group and more like a mission-focused task force. I called it the "Avengers of AI." Like Marvel's superhero team where each member brings unique powers to save the world, we brought together leaders from across departments—engineering, sales, customer success, UX, marketing, and even finance—each bringing their unique departmental superpowers to the mission. The idea wasn't to have each department represented so they could defend their turf but instead to align around a single customer experience and build toward it *together*.

Every member of that team brought different strengths and different ways of thinking. But they all cared deeply about one thing: making it easier for customers to get value quickly. This became the organizing principle. No longer was anyone asking how to protect their current process. Now, suddenly everyone was asking what it would take to deliver results with less friction.

Reimagining the Customer Journey

The team began by mapping the entire customer journey, from first contact to renewal. They examined where handoffs failed, where tools didn't talk to each other, and where customers asked for help again and again. Then they reimagined what the experience could look like if it were built from the ground up using digital tools. Instead of duplicating existing workflows, they streamlined and automated the most time-consuming tasks. They created early prototypes, tested them in real time, and adjusted based on feedback.

The speed of progress surprised the organization. With clear goals and the freedom to experiment, the team moved quickly. The product evolved from a high-touch custom service into a configurable platform that could onboard clients independently. New customers began launching in weeks instead of months, and engineering regained its focus on the core road map. Sales closed deals more confidently, while customer success shifted toward strategic advisory instead of reactive support.

Enablers of Change: Leadership and Empowerment

Leadership supported the effort by removing roadblocks and championing the initiative at every level. They stayed close to the team, encouraged honest feedback, and responded when issues surfaced. That leadership presence created a sense of urgency and permission that allowed the work to thrive.

The breakthrough wasn't the software but the way people came together to build it. Traditional structures had pushed departments to operate in isolation while this model did the opposite. It invited collaboration, supported learning, and made it easier for people to contribute beyond their formal roles. When departments understand each other's goals—and how those goals serve both the external ME (customer) and internal ME (employee)—they can create value faster and with fewer misunderstandings. This dual focus on individual success enabled by organizational capability becomes the foundation for sustainable transformation. And when you can celebrate the small wins, you socialize success, which drives interest and adoption across the organization.

When departments understand each other's goals—and how those goals serve both the external ME (customer) and internal ME (employee)—they can create value faster and with fewer misunderstandings.

The most effective transformation teams start by getting the right voices in the room. Not just the loudest ones or the ones with technical expertise but the ones closest to the customers and the ones willing to challenge assumptions. Simply said, the "Avengers of AI" approach unlocks the potential that already exists within the organization.

The Cross-Functional Transformation Model

If there's one constant in successful digital transformation, it's the structure and dynamics of the team driving it. Not the org chart, not the budget, not the technology stack. It's the cross-functional alignment of people who understand the real work of the business and are empowered to reshape it together. When transformation fails, it's often because teams are built around hierarchy and oversight rather than collaboration and ownership.

The most effective teams bring together voices from across the business. They include operations, IT, data, compliance, and frontline employees. They aren't stacked with specialists who operate in silos. They reflect the full operating system of the company. They see the friction that slows things down, and they understand the tools and insights required to remove it. These teams operate like working models of what the future state should look like. When assembled thoughtfully, these groups function as agile execution engines because each member contributes domain expertise, though their real value comes from how they think together.

Empowerment is central for true cross-functional transformation. These teams must have the authority to make decisions, not just the permission to suggest them, regardless of whether you're building this capability from scratch or enhancing existing collaborative structures. They need access to data and tools and the freedom to test and iterate. More importantly, they need leaders who remove roadblocks and who stay close enough to the work to support momentum without micro-managing it. Without this kind of empowerment, even the best ideas lose traction quickly.

FROM FUNCTION-FIRST TO MISSION-FIRST

Transformation requires a clear shift in mindset, from function-first to mission-first. That means every decision is filtered through the lens of the shared goal and everyone is working toward a single, clearly defined outcome. And those outcomes must be visible, measurable, and relevant, not vague aspirations about becoming more digital. They are tangible results that show up in customer satisfaction, employee engagement, time to market, and revenue.

Another critical shift involves how work is organized. Traditional waterfall planning won't keep up with the pace and complexity of digital initiatives. The age of the flawless blueprint is over. Our only guarantee of success is a commitment to action, data-driven agility, and a willingness to learn first. Instead of large, sequential project phases, these teams adopt agile cycles, operating in sprints and gathering feedback continuously, refining ideas in motion. This iterative approach allows for faster course corrections and earlier value delivery.

Our only guarantee of success is a commitment to action, data-driven agility, and a willingness to learn first.

TOOLS THAT SUPPORT AGILE TRANSFORMATION

To support this way of working, structure matters. A simple but powerful tool is the mission brief. It outlines the objective, the metrics that define success, and the timeline for delivery. It's short, but it creates alignment. It gives every team member clarity on what matters most and how their contribution connects to the larger mission.

Agile rituals help enforce that alignment. Daily scrums keep the team connected, while demos provide moments to share progress and gather feedback. And retrospectives make it easier to improve both the product and the process. These are habits that keep the team grounded in shared ownership and continuous learning.

Visibility is also essential across the organization. Transformation teams must work in the open, sharing updates not just with each other but with adjacent departments and leadership. Shared dashboards can help here because they allow anyone to see what's being built, what progress is being made, and what outcomes are being measured. This kind of transparency creates trust, which turns the work of transformation from a hidden initiative into a shared journey.

The best cross-functional teams demonstrate what a more aligned, agile, and empowered organization can look like. They model a future in which ideas move faster, silos shrink, and people feel connected to the outcomes they're driving.

The best cross-functional teams demonstrate what a more aligned, agile, and empowered organization can look like.

This effect becomes even more powerful in AI-driven transformation, where the pace of change demands continuous adaptation. In my experience, the real breakthrough isn't just about the technology itself but about how people collaborate around it. Over time, these teams create a new kind of institutional knowledge; they build the collaborative muscle memory your organization needs to not only keep pace but *evolve* with each new technological wave.

The data backs this up:

- Fifty-five percent of teams that use AI and automation tools report they're able to take on more work, and 90 percent are more likely to report having opportunities to do meaningful work.[4]

---

4   Microsoft WorkLab, *Work Trend Index Annual Report: 2025: The Year the Frontier Firm Is Born* (Microsoft, 2025), https://www.microsoft.com/en-us/worklab/work-trend-index/2025-the-year-the-frontier-firm-is-born.

- Organizations that invest in technology to support teamwork have seen a 27 percent increase in sales and 30 percent improvement in product development.[5]
- Companies that successfully implement effective change management—a key component of collaboration—achieve 143 percent of their expected ROI, while those that don't only achieve 35 percent.[6]

This shows that technology is only as good as the teams who wield it.

Building Team Agility Through Psychological Safety

If you want speed, you need safety. That may sound counterintuitive, but in every successful digital transformation I've seen, the cultural foundation mattered as much as the technical framework. No team can operate at full velocity without a shared sense of trust. When people fear consequences for speaking candidly or experimenting openly, innovation gets smothered before it starts.

Let's be clear about the definition of psychological safety. In the context of digital transformation, psychological safety means creating an environment in which teams can challenge assumptions, surface issues, and contribute ideas without fear of embarrassment or retali-

---

5   Forrester, *The Total Economic Impact™ of Microsoft Teams, Improved Employee and Company Performance* (Forrester, 2019), https://www.microsoft.com/en-us/ microsoft-365/blog/wp-content/uploads/sites/2/2019/04/Total-Economic-Impact- Microsoft-Teams.pdf.

6   Jennifer A. LaClair and Ravi P. Rao, "Helping Employees Embrace Change," *McKinsey Quarterly*, November 1, 2002, https://www.mckinsey. com/capabilities/people-and-organizational-performance/our-insights/ helping-employees-embrace-change.

ation. In high-performing teams, it's not risky to say "I don't know," or to suggest a half-baked idea. It's part of the work.

Too many transformation efforts falter because fear takes up too much space. People hold back, waiting to be told what to do. They become experts in looking busy rather than being bold. A culture that prizes perfection and punishes missteps is a culture that will struggle to evolve.

A culture that prizes perfection and punishes missteps is a culture that will struggle to evolve.

Contrast that with environments in which reflection is routine. In agile teams, retrospectives happen regularly, not just when things go wrong. These moments are built into the rhythm of delivery to get to the bottom of what worked and what needs to change before the next cycle begins.

Language matters here too. Oftentimes, without realizing it, leaders set the tone. If experimentation is talked about like a last resort or a risk to be mitigated, teams won't embrace it. But when "test and learn" is woven into how work is described, it becomes normal to iterate, to adapt quickly, and to view setbacks as sources of insight rather than failures.

We had two clients facing the same market shift.

Client A was a leader in their industry, but they were hesitant to experiment. While they had been consistently hitting all their topline numbers—albeit barely—for over six quarters, their incentives were tied to maintaining the status quo, not to risk-taking. The executives were too focused on incremental improvements to maintain the numbers and didn't take the time to truly understand the changing tech landscape. Their mindset was, "I'm too busy, and the technology isn't ready for prime time, so I'll just wait." They were so focused on avoiding failure that they missed the opportunity to learn. Eventually, their competitor, Client B, leapfrogged them.

Client B, on the other hand, wasn't afraid to be scrappy. We launched a small, low-risk test—a new feature on their website that could be turned off with a single click. It wasn't perfect, and the first version failed. But we learned from it. We analyzed the data, adjusted, and launched a second version. Then a third. Each iteration brought us closer to a real breakthrough, which ultimately led to a new product line and a significant revenue stream. They embraced the mindset that a small failure today is an essential lesson for a major success tomorrow.

The lesson here is that a "fast follower" mindset will lead to complacency. By the time you're ready to react, your more experimental and nimble-minded competitors will have already created a gap that's impossible to close. Customers go where they see consistent value driven to them. They don't care about your complacency.

CULTURAL MARKERS OF PSYCHOLOGICAL SAFETY

One of the best indicators of cultural health is what happens in meetings. When ideas flow freely, when people are willing to disagree, when there's laughter and challenge in equal measure, that's a sign the team feels safe. But when meetings are dominated by silence and people nod along without engagement, those are warning signs. Something is being held back.

Another red flag is how problems are surfaced. In agile environments, issues are elevated early, often, and without drama. There's no reward for hiding them. But when people hesitate to escalate, or when leaders react defensively to feedback, problems linger. And ultimately trust degrades.

Psychological safety—essentially building a workplace where people feel safe to speak up, try new things, and admit mistakes—also plays a role in how teams absorb change. Digital transformation doesn't just shift systems; it shifts roles, processes, and power dynamics. Without a foundation of safety, these shifts create anxiety. With it, teams are more resilient and view change as something to shape, not something to survive.

Creating this kind of environment requires intentionality, beginning with leaders who model the behavior they want to see. That means showing vulnerability, owning mistakes, and asking for input, especially from those closest to the work.

Agility only grows from this kind of soil. When people feel trusted, they take initiative. When they know their voice matters, they speak up sooner. And when failure is treated as data, not a demerit, learning accelerates.

Governance: The Race Car of AI

Successful digital transformation depends on leadership that goes beyond initiating change. It demands clarity, consistency, and the courage to stay involved. At its best, leadership aligns vision with execution and ensures that governance empowers rather than inhibits.

Every transformation starts with a clear sense of purpose. That vision must be articulated not just as an aspiration but as a strategic direction grounded in business outcomes. Leaders define the future state and translate it into tangible, operational intent. Without this clarity, teams struggle to make aligned decisions, and progress becomes fragmented.

But vision without sponsorship falls short. Too many initiatives suffer from passive leadership, where the vision is stated once and then left to drift. In contrast, effective sponsors stay visible. They support the cross-functional teams, not by micromanaging but by protecting their focus, clearing obstacles, and giving them the air cover needed to execute.

To lead transformation well, executives must also model the mindset they expect from others. That includes openness to change, adaptability under pressure, and a willingness to learn. Culture, as we know, cascades from the top. When senior leaders demonstrate curiosity and humility, it grants others permission to do the same. But strong leadership also means actively managing stakeholders at every level, ensuring that people understand why change is happening, what's in it for them, and how it ultimately benefits the customer. It also means rethinking governance not as a rubber stamp or a final gatekeeper but as an enabler. Effective governance becomes a mechanism for sharing knowledge about what works and what doesn't, for applying new innovations consistently across the organization, and for safeguarding the elements that matter most—brand integrity, customer trust, and data privacy. Leaders who embrace this expanded role create clarity, momentum, and alignment in the face of ongoing change.

This cultural foundation feeds directly into how governance is structured. Think of AI as a high-powered race car. Governance is both the driver and the rules of the road. The car may be capable of extraordinary speed and complexity, but without a driver who understands how to control it, and rules that prevent it from veering off course, it becomes a risk rather than an asset. As the driver, governance provides strategic direction. It keeps the organization aligned with ethical principles and business goals. This includes determining the destination, selecting the optimal path, and knowing when to accelerate or slow down, applying judgment in real time based on data, context, and experience.

Governance also serves as a protective framework. It ensures fairness, transparency, and accountability. Like race regulations designed to prevent accidents, these principles exist not to constrain speed but to preserve integrity and safety as innovation scales. Responsible AI systems require oversight that is proactive, not punitive. Humans must be involved not only in the design but throughout the lifecycle, validating data, monitoring performance, and intervening when necessary.

EMBEDDING GOVERNANCE INTO THE WORK

Too often, governance becomes a bottleneck. A committee sits outside the work, tasked with reviewing and approving everything. This slows decisions and ultimately separates the people responsible for outcomes from the authority to deliver them. That cumbersome model doesn't serve modern transformation.

Instead, governance must be reimagined as a support structure embedded within the work itself. Governance should guide, not gatekeep. It should clarify ethical boundaries, ensure regulatory compliance, and maintain visibility, but it should do so from within the transformation team, not from across the hall.

Governance should guide, not gatekeep.

When done well, governance helps create a safe space to move quickly and responsibly. It sets clear expectations around transparency, fairness, and accountability, then allows teams to operate within those boundaries.

AI Governance: The Cornerstone of Responsible Transformation

In any significant transformation effort, governance is the linchpin between ambition and execution. When you fold AI into the mix, the stakes are even higher. The systems we deploy today go beyond automating tasks to shape decisions, influence behavior, and carry real consequences for individuals and communities. Without a thoughtful, deliberate governance model, even the best-intentioned AI initiatives can go off course.

PRINCIPLES OF RESPONSIBLE AI GOVERNANCE

One of the most urgent responsibilities of AI governance is ensuring ethical alignment. Algorithms, for all their efficiency, are not inherently fair. They learn from historical data, which often carries the same biases and blind spots that society has failed to address. Without checks in place, AI systems can perpetuate discrimination, marginalize vulnerable populations, or make decisions that are misaligned with organizational values. A robust governance model doesn't leave ethics to chance. It embeds them from the start by defining what responsible AI use looks like, setting boundaries around acceptable use cases, and creating mechanisms for continuous reflection and adjustment.

Risk is another unavoidable reality. AI introduces new forms of uncertainty, from unintended outputs to data vulnerabilities. It can obscure decision-making, making it harder to pinpoint the cause of a bad outcome. That's why strong AI governance includes a dedicated risk management framework. This involves identifying potential points of failure and setting clear thresholds for when and how intervention should occur. It also means assigning responsibility.

Someone needs to own the risks and have the authority to act before small problems escalate.

Compliance is evolving alongside AI. New regulations are being introduced in nearly every sector—from the European Union's General Data Protection Regulation (GDPR, a comprehensive data privacy law that took effect in 2018) to proposed federal frameworks in the US and elsewhere. These rules govern everything from data privacy to algorithmic fairness, and the pace of change is only accelerating. A forward-looking governance model ensures that AI systems not only meet current standards but are built to adapt as regulations evolve.

A forward-looking governance model ensures that AI systems not only meet current standards but are built to adapt as regulations evolve.

Trust is a prerequisite for adoption, whether for customers, employees, or partners. People need to understand how AI systems work and why they should rely on them. That's why transparency and explainability must be foundational to any governance model. Make inputs, algorithms, and outputs comprehensible to nonexperts. If a customer asks why a recommendation was made, or an employee wonders how a tool is prioritizing their workflow, there should be a clear, accurate explanation available. Every system must be human-readable and auditable.

Accountability also extends beyond transparency. AI governance must clarify who is responsible for what during development, deployment, and everyday use. This includes technical teams, business leaders, and anyone interacting with the AI system. Contrary to popular belief, accountability is about clarity, not blame. Everyone involved should know their role, understand how their decisions impact the system, and have the tools to fulfill their responsibilities.

OPERATIONALIZING GOVERNANCE AT SCALE

A governance model also needs to support scale. As AI becomes more embedded in business operations, the challenge is in creating repeatable processes for data sourcing, model development, performance validation, and ongoing monitoring. It also means ensuring that as AI expands into new departments or use cases, the principles of ethical alignment, risk management, and transparency go with it.

This kind of AI governance can't be a standalone function. It must be deeply embedded within transformation efforts, not layered on top after decisions have already been made. It should operate as a set of guiding practices, visible and accessible to every team building, deploying, or relying on AI systems. And it must evolve continuously, just as the technology does.

The organizations that will lead in the age of AI are the ones that move fast but with care and clarity. Confidence is cultivated by people who are empowered and equipped to navigate what's next. Governance sets the direction, but it's the people who drive the change.

That's why the next chapter turns to the most vital element of transformation: preparing your workforce to lead, adapt, and thrive in a world where digital fluency is no longer optional but essential.

FIVE STEPS TO TAKE NOW

Breaking down silos is an operational necessity. Without collaboration, alignment, and psychological safety, digital transformation loses traction before it ever reaches the customer. But this kind of change doesn't begin with restructuring org charts or hiring more consultants. It begins with intentional action, taken consistently, by leaders willing to model what agility looks like.

These five steps are grounded in what I've seen work across organizations of every size and industry.

Step 1: Create a Cross-Functional "Mission Brief"

Bring together six to eight leaders or practitioners from different departments—engineering, operations, sales, marketing, finance, and frontline roles. Frame the session with one outcome in mind: clarity.

Ask the group to coauthor a one-page "mission brief" that answers these questions:

- What customer experience are we trying to improve?
- What outcome defines success?
- What does progress look like over the next thirty days?

This single artifact becomes a reference point for every decision, keeping diverse teams aligned without requiring constant escalation.

Step 2: Map a Broken Handoff

Choose one process where responsibilities shift between departments, such as onboarding a new customer, launching a feature, or responding to a service issue. Bring the teams involved together to map what currently happens and where it breaks down.

Ask:

- What are the unspoken expectations?
- Where does information get lost?
- What would make this transition seamless for the customer?

You don't need software to fix a handoff. You need visibility, shared understanding, and agreement on what good looks like.

Step 3: Run a Psychological Safety Check

In your next team meeting, take five minutes to gather honest feedback on how people feel about three simple prompts:

- I feel safe sharing rough ideas here.
- When something isn't working, I can say so without fear.
- If I take a risk and it fails, I'll be supported.

Use anonymous polling if needed. Look at the responses not as performance data but as cultural indicators. If you score low, don't panic ... *get curious*. Ask what needs to change to foster greater safety and trust.

Step 4: Launch a Two-Week Collaboration Sprint

Pick a high-friction area and assemble a small, empowered team to address it over the next two weeks. Give them three things:

1. A clear goal tied to customer or business value
2. Freedom to experiment
3. Direct access to a senior sponsor who can clear roadblocks

Schedule a midpoint check-in and a final demo to leadership. The goal isn't to solve everything. It's to show what's possible when alignment, autonomy, and speed converge.

Step 5: Redefine Governance as a Support Function

Take one policy, approval process, or oversight mechanism that currently slows down innovation, and redesign it to accelerate trust instead of delay progress.

Ask:

- Is this protecting value or just preserving precedent?
- Can we embed this control closer to the work?
- What does responsible speed look like here?

Even small changes—such as clarifying decision rights or simplifying approvals—can make a meaningful difference in how fast your teams can move with confidence.

CHAPTER FOUR

EQUIPPING YOUR PEOPLE FOR THE DIGITAL AGE

Technology is nothing. What's important is that you have a faith in people, that they're basically good and smart, and if you give them tools, they'll do wonderful things with them.

—STEVE JOBS

Your Mission Possible Blueprint: Your people are your greatest asset, but only if they're equipped for what's coming. This chapter provides a framework for building digital capability that scales. By the end, you'll have five concrete steps to begin developing the workforce your future business requires.

WHEN IT COMES to building digital fluency across a team or an entire organization, most people start in the wrong place. They dive into courses and pilot tools, maybe roll out some generic "AI for Everyone" workshops. It feels like momentum, but it's usually noise.

If you want real change, if you want to actually equip people to thrive in a digital-first world, you have to start with defining what the future looks like and why it matters.

That's where True North comes in. I use that phrase deliberately because it forces clarity. It's not about where your team is today, but where you *need them to be* for the business to grow, adapt, and stay relevant. You can't get there by asking, What are we doing now, and how do we do it better? You get there by asking, Where is the business going, and what will we need to be capable of when we get there?

One of the biggest mistakes I see is when leaders simply project current processes forward. They take today's job descriptions and try to retrofit training around them. But the roles themselves are evolving. The tools are changing. The expectations customers and employees have are shifting fast.

Companies contemplating a foray into generative AI should let someone else make the tools. That's the takeaway from a recent MIT study, which found that 95 percent of internal AI pilot programs fail to boost revenue or productivity.[7] According to Fortune, the issue isn't subpar models but flawed integration.[8] Successful startups use AI to solve targeted problems, with specialized external vendors succeeding twice as often as proprietary pilots. The MIT study (based on 150 interviews with leaders, a survey of 350 employees, and an analysis of 300 public AI deployments) also determined that too much AI spend goes to sales and marketing, even though reducing outsourcing and

---

7   Aditya Challapally et al., *The GenAI Divide: State of AI in Business 2025* (MIT NANDA, 2025), https://mlq.ai/media/quarterly_decks/v0.1_State_of_AI_in_Business_2025_Report.pdf.

8   Jeremy Kahn, "An MIT Report That 95% of AI Pilots Fail Spooked Investors. But It's the Reason Why Those Pilots Failed That Should Make the C-Suite Anxious," *Fortune*, August 21, 2025, https://fortune.com/2025/08/21/an-mit-report-that-95-of-ai-pilots-fail-spooked-investors-but-the-reason-why-those-pilots-failed-is-what-should-make-the-c-suite-anxious/.

streamlining back-office operations drive savings. This means they were delivering little to no measurable impact on P&L, according to *Forbes*.[9]

Even more telling, purchasing AI tools from specialized vendors and building partnerships succeeds two-thirds of the time, while internal builds succeed only one-third as often.[10]

That gap is less about the quality of model output and more about proper change management. You can't just roll out generic tools and expect employees to adapt their workflows.

ESCAPING AI PILOT PURGATORY

It's a sobering statistic: Over 90 percent of AI pilots fail. But in my experience, that failure isn't about the technology itself. It's about a failure of strategy. These projects land in "purgatory"—a place where a cool idea never graduates to a real business solution—because leaders don't ask the right questions at the outset.

To avoid being in the 90 percent, you need to shift your mindset from simply exploring AI to intentionally building with it. Here are my recommendations for leaders:

Design for Scale from Day One

In AWS, we learned that a service must be designed for scale from the very beginning. The same is true for AI. Don't build a pilot in a closed sandbox that works for one team and one workflow. Instead, build a proof of concept

---

9   Arafat Kabir, "MIT Report Says AI Is Failing. But What If We Are Measuring Wrong?" *Forbes*, August 26, 2025, https://www.forbes.com/sites/arafatkabir/2025/08/26/mit-report-says-ai-is-failing-but-what-if-we-are-measuring-wrong/.

10   Challapally et al., *The GenAI Divide*.

that connects to a real data source, real users, and a real business problem. Ask yourself: Can this solution handle a tenfold or hundredfold increase in volume? If the answer isn't clear, you're building a toy, not a tool.

Anchor to a Measurable Outcome

Many AI pilots chase a "shiny object" without a clear purpose. It's like building a new type of server but not knowing what you'll run on it. Your pilot should be tied to a measurable, high-value business outcome. Is the goal to increase sales by 5 percent? Reduce customer churn by 10 percent? Shorten the average customer service call by thirty seconds? When the outcome is clear, you can rally your teams around a tangible goal and demonstrate its value.

Build for Integration, Not Isolation

The most powerful thing about the cloud is its composability. Each service, from S3 to Lambda, is designed to work together. Your AI pilots must be the same. Avoid a one-off, siloed project. Ensure your pilot is built with a clear path to integrate with your existing legacy systems and workflows. If it requires a massive, onetime overhaul of your infrastructure, it will never get off the ground.

By following these principles, you can shift from a reactive, experimental approach to a proactive, intentional one. You move beyond building proofs of concept that die in a demo to building foundations that can support an entire new era of your business.

So, how do you avoid becoming another failed AI case study? Build a culture that rewards adoption and experimentation. Invest in employee training by committing time and resources. Develop tools with employees, not just for them.

Skip any of these steps and you risk becoming another statistic.

Scan this QR code to access the Insights Hub and find my Digital Transformation Playbook: 7 Critical Focus Areas. If you train people for today's pain points, you'll be caught off guard tomorrow. So before you schedule a single training, start by answering this: What does tenfold look like?

If you train people for today's pain points, you'll be caught off guard tomorrow.

The Tenfold Test

If your department had to handle ten times the output, ten times the customers, or ten times the complexity, what would break first? Where would friction show up? What kinds of decisions would people need to make faster and with better data? And how would their roles need to change in order to stay effective? These questions help you form a picture of the future operating model. They help leaders visualize what success will actually require. That clarity is critical because it directly shapes the kind of digital capability you need to build.

Let's say your HR team today runs workforce planning using spreadsheets and quarterly meetings—or say HR has already adopted some digital tools. Either way you cut it, transformative leaders must constantly ask themselves whether the systems, processes, and tools their teams use are being leveraged to their fullest potential. Maybe your current tools work at your current size, but they won't work in a transformative business that operates with real-time data and distributed teams. The future version of that HR team needs fluency in analytics tools, an understanding of how to evaluate and act on talent signals, and yes, a comfort level with AI-supported decision making. The same is true for marketing, finance, operations—every department. Roles don't disappear, but they do evolve. And digital acumen becomes part of the job, not an add-on.

This is future-back thinking, like Amazon's philosophy of working backward from the desired future state in eighteen months. To get there, ask yourself what must change, be eliminated, be reengineered, or be reimagined. It might sound abstract, but it's not if it is grounded in real conversations. Sit down with department leaders. Ask what success looks like in eighteen months, not what hurts right now. Spend time mapping what their work could become with the right tools and the right skills. Invite them to imagine what would need to change if they had to deliver their best work faster, with fewer handoffs, and more data-informed insight. That exercise often surfaces gaps you didn't know existed.

And don't skip the step of listening to the people closest to the work. Frontline teams will often tell you, in plain terms, where processes fall apart or where tools are getting in the way. They'll also show you where they've improvised and created manual workarounds, built their own tracking systems, or found ways to collaborate that aren't in the playbook. Those signals matter. They show you where the current state is brittle and where better tools alone won't solve the problem. Often, the real constraint is confidence or capacity, not availability of technology.

This kind of diagnosis takes time. It might feel slow, especially when the pressure to upskill fast is everywhere. But I promise, this is how you speed up later. If you take the time to define where you're going and what success will look like when you get there, the training becomes obvious. You're no longer guessing what to teach. You're building capabilities that are connected to real goals. And when people can see how their learning is tied to the future of the business, and their role in it, they're a lot more likely to engage, apply it, and help shape what's next.

When people can see how their learning is tied to the future of the business, and their role in it, they're a lot more likely to engage, apply it, and help shape what's next.

Diagnosing the Gap

Once you've defined your digital True North, the next step is to figure out where you're starting. That sounds obvious, but most organizations do it wrong. They'll run a quick survey, collect a few stats on who attended training, and call it a baseline. But diagnosing a digital skills gap means revealing what's really happening inside your teams—the hidden friction, the workarounds no one wants to admit to, the missed signals in the systems you already have. And you won't find any of that in a dashboard alone.

Start with conversations. Real ones. Pull together focus groups with frontline employees, team leads, and department heads. Ask them to walk you through how work actually gets done. What tools do they use day to day? What feels cumbersome? Where do they copy and paste data between systems just to move things forward? These details matter, because they expose the difference between what's been deployed and what's actually being used. Most tools look great on paper. But only when you observe how teams interact with them in real life do you see the disconnect.

You're listening for a few specific signals. Manual workarounds are usually the first clue. If someone has to open five browser tabs and pull three reports just to answer a basic customer question, something's broken. If team members are exporting data from one system to plug it into their own tracking sheet because the official tool is too clunky or confusing, that's not innovation; it's a symptom. It tells you people aren't being set up for success, and they're finding workarounds to cope.

Then there are the bottlenecks. These show up as persistent friction in processes that should flow smoothly—approvals that stall out, reports that take too long to compile, decisions that sit in limbo while someone waits for the right data. When teams hit these slowdowns repeatedly, it's often because they don't have the fluency or confidence to use the tools available to them. Or worse, the tools themselves don't actually align with how people work. And for the record, throwing bodies at bottlenecks almost always fails. You don't need heroes who dive in to solve problems like bottlenecks. You need heroes who do the work ahead of time to ensure you don't need heroes.

Another red flag is underutilized data. In too many organizations, critical decisions are still made by gut feel or habit instead of insight. The dashboards exist. The reports are there. But no one's using them to inform strategy. That's not a data problem; it's a fluency problem. It tells you people either don't trust the data, don't understand how to apply it, or don't believe it's worth the effort to figure out. Or, after years of comfort doing it their way, they believe a new way can't possibly teach them something they don't already know. I see the pervasiveness of this detrimental mentality. This is an issue that usually comes back to how tools are introduced, taught, and supported.

Once you've surfaced those signals, dig into the *why*. Behind every stalled transformation is a mix of structural and psychological barriers. Lack of training is a big one but not the only one. Some teams feel overwhelmed by constant tool changes. Others have been burned by past rollouts that promised big improvements but delivered more complexity. There's also fear of looking slow, of being replaced, of not having time to learn something new without dropping the ball on current work. And then there's the classic corporate shell game, where accountability gets passed around until it disappears. If a leader treats digital upskilling as someone else's problem, don't expect their team to embrace it either.

Behind every stalled transformation is a mix of structural and psychological barriers.

To move forward, you need to document what you're seeing in a structured way. That's where a skills matrix comes in. This isn't a twenty-page spreadsheet of everything a person could possibly learn. It's a high-level map of the capabilities your future state requires compared to what your teams can do today. Think in terms of key workflows and decisions: What tools should be in regular use? What kind of data literacy is required? Where do human judgment and creativity need to be supported, not replaced, by technology?

Once you've built that map, you can start to prioritize. And this part is crucial. You can't (and shouldn't) try to upskill everyone on everything all at once. That's how people tune out. Focus instead on what drives the biggest impact. Which roles or teams are closest to the customer, or at the center of revenue-generating activity? Where would a boost in fluency create the most immediate lift in efficiency or experience? Then sequence the work. Think in terms of small, digestible steps. One workflow. One tool. One outcome at a time.

This approach builds credibility. It shows people that training isn't just something being handed down from corporate. It's targeted, relevant, and designed to make their work better, faster, and more rewarding. When teams start to see that connection, resistance drops and adoption grows.

If you're already leveraging similar tools in your own workflows, you know the real breakthrough isn't the speed, it's the shift in thinking. Using AI for the mindless details allows us to be more mindful about what really matters. It enables our human capacity, and as the technology continues to evolve, so too will our ability to focus on strategy, relationships, and innovation.

The crucial first step is to get your team to embrace the new tools. That happens when they see the value for themselves, not just for the company. The numbers are clear:

- **Relevance drives engagement.** A study by HR Drive found that 91 percent of employees want personalized training that is relevant to their specific role, and 93 percent prefer training that is easy to complete.[11] When training isn't just something handed down from corporate but is targeted and designed to make work better, faster, and more rewarding, resistance drops and adoption grows.

- **Engagement leads to productivity.** A Gallup survey shows that companies with engaged employees are 21 percent more profitable and 17 percent more productive.[12] Personalized training is a key driver of that engagement, and studies show that employees who feel their company invests in their learning are 47 percent less likely to look for a new job.[13]

- **Personalization creates momentum.** "A case study of a global specialty materials company found that AI-enhanced learning solutions improved operational efficiency by up to 15%, [and] increased productivity by up to 20%."[14] This shows that when teams start to see a real connection between new tools and their personal growth, the momentum builds, leading to meaningful business outcomes.

Then and only then will the momentum build.

---

11 Riia O'Donnell, "Why Traditional Classroom Training Isn't Enough for Today's Employee," HRDive.com, March 6, 2018, https://www.hrdive.com/news/why-traditional-classroom-training-isnt-enough-for-todays-employee/518229/.

12 Brandon Rigoni and Bailey Nelson, "Do Employees Really Know What's Expected of Them?" Gallup, September 27, 2016, https://news.gallup.com/businessjournal/195803/employees-really-know-expected.aspx.

13 Gallup and Workhuman, *The Human-Centered Workplace: Building Organizational Cultures that Thrive* (Gallup, 2024), https://www.gallup.com/analytics/472658/workplace-recognition-research.aspx.

14 Aaron Teitelbaum, "The Future of Work Is Personal: How AI Is Reshaping Employee Experience," *SHRM*, February 27, 2025, https://www.shrm.org/enterprise-solutions/insights/future-of-work-is-personal-how-ai-is-reshaping-employee.

Surfacing the Invisible: Using AI to Reveal Skill Gaps and Learning Needs

Even with the best interviews, focus groups, and diagnostics, some signals stay buried. People don't always know what they don't know. And even when they do, they won't always say it out loud. That's where AI steps in as a layer that brings clarity to the gaps we can't always see or articulate.

The first place to look is behavior. Not what people claim they're doing but what their actions actually show. Behavioral analytics— tracking what people actually do versus what they say they do—cut through the perception fog. If you're rolling out a CRM, you want to know: Are your sales reps logging follow-ups in the system, or are they still tracking them in a private spreadsheet? If the team has access to automated reports, are they using them to guide decisions, or are they relying on outdated manual exports? These are simple questions that most organizations answer with guesses. AI gives you something better. It gives you *truth*.

By tracking real-time tool usage within your CRM, enterprise resource planning, collaboration platforms, and project management systems, you start to get a picture of actual digital engagement, not to count the clicks or log-ins but to understand how people interact with systems across time. Are they using the features designed to simplify their work? Or are they sticking to legacy workflows inside modern tools, just going through the motions? That behavior tells you more than a survey ever could.

And when you compare usage patterns with performance data, the real story starts to emerge. Maybe your top-performing customer service reps consistently access knowledge base articles or use AI-generated summaries to close tickets faster. Maybe the lagging team in another region avoids those features entirely. That's a signal of not just where gaps exist, but how those gaps translate into missed outcomes. You begin to see which capabilities actually drive business results, and where targeted support would move the needle.

When you compare usage patterns with performance data, the real story starts to emerge.

This doesn't stop at system logs. AI-powered natural language processing can help you mine the qualitative side—the open-ended feedback, internal chats, email summaries, and Slack threads. That's where signs of confusion, frustration, or resistance show up first. "This tool's clunky." "I'm not sure what this dashboard means." "It's easier if I just do it the old way." When you aggregate that input across teams and platforms, patterns begin to surface. You see not only where people struggle but how they talk about the struggle. That sentiment matters because it shapes adoption long before training begins.

Now you can start to customize the path forward. Personalized learning isn't about creating a thousand bespoke courses. It's about recognizing that not every team, or even every role, needs the same depth of knowledge in every tool. The finance department might need hands-on simulations for AI-driven forecasting. The marketing team might need more time with sentiment analysis modules or tools for automated content optimization. By analyzing how different teams engage with digital systems, you can tailor training to what matters most for each.

And this is where simulation and gamification play a role. Static tutorials and compliance videos won't cut it. If you want to know whether someone can apply a tool in the real world, let them practice in a scenario that mimics the actual task. These simulations can be scored, refined, and repeated, giving both the learner and the organization feedback on progress. When the assessments feel like challenges instead of chores, engagement goes up. So does retention. And more importantly, you get an honest read on who's ready, who needs support, and what kind of enablement will actually work.

Think of AI here as your listening system. It captures the signals people don't always voice. It connects behavior to outcomes. And it gives you the intelligence to design interventions that are timely, relevant, and grounded in reality. You no longer have to guess where the gaps are, or worse, wait until they derail progress. You can see them early and act with precision.

Mindset Over Metrics

You can have the best training program in the world, but if your people think it's a prelude to being replaced, they won't engage. They'll smile, nod, and find a way to stay in their comfort zone. The reality is that fear is one of the most persistent blockers to digital adoption, and much of that fear is inadvertently triggered by leadership language.

Fear is one of the most persistent blockers to digital adoption, and much of that fear is inadvertently triggered by leadership language.

Too many transformation efforts still default to the vocabulary of efficiency—streamlining, automation, productivity gains. And while those may be valid business outcomes, they don't inspire confidence in your workforce. Efficiency is often heard as code for cuts. People start to do the math. If this new AI tool saves me 40 percent of my time, what happens to the other 60 percent? When you lead with metrics, you invite defensive behavior. What you need instead is a mindset reset. One that frames the digital shift as an opportunity to expand, not eliminate, human contribution.

Start by being deliberate in how you position AI. Make it clear that the goal is partnership, not replacement. AI doesn't take your job; it takes the grind out of your job. It handles the tedious, the repetitive, and the mechanical so that your time can be spent where judgment, creativity, and connection matter most. That message must be more than a slide in a town hall. It has to come through consistently from leadership, reinforced in day-to-day conversations and in the decisions leaders make.

The true power of this shift is how it changes the nature of work. I once saw a team of customer service agents who spent a significant portion of their day manually filling out forms and navigating clunky systems. After implementing a simple AI tool that automated these tasks, they suddenly had an extra hour each day. Instead of using that time to take on more rote work, they used it to connect with customers, build stronger relationships, and solve more complex, rewarding problems. They became proactive, not just reactive. The automation didn't replace their jobs; it freed them up to do the work they actually cared about—the work that gave them new, more impactful skills and delighted customers.

If you're a senior executive, you have to model digital curiosity. You need to be seen asking questions, trying new tools, and occasionally getting it wrong in public. That's how you build psychological safety. If people think their leaders are infallible and uninterested in learning, they'll assume failure isn't allowed for them either. And nothing kills innovation faster than that.

When I speak to teams, I often use the hockey puck analogy. The great players don't skate to where the puck is, they skate to where it's *going to be*. That's how you think about digital skill building. Don't train for the tools you used last year. Train for the problems you're going to face next year.

The true power of this shift is how it changes the nature of work. Think about elevators. People forget that before elevators, we built outward. Cities were low and sprawling. Once the elevator arrived, everything changed. The skyline evolved. Not because the elevator alone was magic, but because people learned to trust it, design around it, and imagine new possibilities because of it.

AI is our elevator moment. It's what lets us rise, *if* we can help people feel safe stepping inside. The focus is not on employee training but on a broader strategic point: how to inspire an organization to embrace transformative change. The elevator metaphor is perfect for this because it's not just about a single tool; it's about the fundamental shift in mindset that an entire society had to make to reap the benefits of that new tool.

AI is our elevator moment. It's what lets us rise, if we can help people feel safe stepping inside.

I also talk about Thanksgiving dinner. Imagine inviting people over and not setting the table. No plates, no silverware, no explanation. Just food. People would feel awkward, confused, and maybe a little resentful. That's what it's like to push digital change without helping people understand how to engage with it. You have to set the table. You have to make the learning approachable, digestible, and clearly connected to what matters in their world.

This shift from compliance to empowerment is critical. If your training program exists just to check a box, your team will treat it that way. They'll complete the modules, but they won't adopt the mindset. But if you position it as a personal and professional growth opportunity, you'll flip the switch and they'll start to lean in.

So the message is simple, but it needs to be consistent: We're not here to measure how fast you complete a course. We're here to help you grow, adapt, and succeed in a world that's changing fast. The technology is evolving. So are our customers. So must we.

Avoiding the Five Classic Pitfalls in Digital Upskilling

When organizations invest in digital training and it still doesn't stick, it's usually not because people aren't smart or willing. It's because the playbook was flawed. Over the years, I've seen the same five pitfalls show up again and again, and I've found they're avoidable if you know how to spot them.

Pitfall one: Chasing the puck. This is the classic mistake of investing in skills for where the business is today rather than where it's headed. It's like training your players to skate only to where the puck is now, ignoring where the play is developing. I see this in companies that finally roll out Excel training just as they're about to adopt AI-powered forecasting tools. Or when teams are trained to master legacy CRMs that are already halfway out the door. The right question isn't, What skills are we missing now? It's, What capabilities will we need in a year or two? If you're only skating to the puck's current location, you'll always be one play behind.

Pitfall two: One-size-fits-all skates. Not everyone in your organization needs the same training. Giving everyone the same set of modules and calling it a digital transformation is like handing out the same sized hockey skates to every player regardless of their position or foot size. It doesn't fit anyone properly, and nobody performs at their best. A finance team needs different tools and techniques than a marketing team. A frontline manager may need hands-on practice with mobile collaboration tools, while a senior strategist may benefit more from scenario modeling or generative AI prompts for analysis. If you don't tailor your approach by function and fluency, you risk disengagement at best and irrelevance at worst.

Pitfall three: Lack of vision connection. This one's a killer. Leaders sometimes assume that people will naturally understand why a new training initiative matters. But without a clear connection between digital upskilling and the organization's broader mission, employees see training as a hoop to jump through, not a lever to pull. They also need to see, feel, and understand what's in it for the employee ME. If you're going to ask people to learn new skills, you have to explain how those skills enable the future you're trying to build. What does success look like after this training is applied? What problems does it help solve? How does it make the work more meaningful or effective? If you don't tie training to vision, it becomes noise. And noise gets tuned out.

Pitfall four: No senior puck-handling. You can't delegate transformation to HR or IT and expect it to land. Upskilling isn't a back-office initiative, it's a frontline leadership priority. If there's no visible support from the top, employees take the cue. They see it as optional or unimportant. And if leaders aren't modeling digital curiosity or engaging with the training themselves, the message is loud and clear. They'll follow your actions, not your slide decks. When I work with executive teams, I always stress this: You don't need to be the expert, but you do need to be engaged. People need to see that leadership is in the rink, not just watching from the press box. And they need to see consistent unwavering alignment.

Pitfall five: DIY learning traps. There's a trend I've seen in some organizations that's well-intentioned but misguided. Leaders say, "We've created a library of learning resources. Our teams can explore and self-direct." That sounds empowering, but in practice, it's like handing out hockey sticks and saying, "Good luck out there." Self-directed learning only works when there's structure, guidance, and psychological safety in place. Without that, most people will stick with what they know. They'll avoid the risk of looking inexperienced. They won't raise their hand to say, "I don't understand this tool" or, "I'm not sure how to apply it." And without that honesty, growth doesn't happen.

If these pitfalls sound familiar, don't worry. Awareness is the first step toward fixing them.

A TALE OF TWO TEAMS

I once worked with a company's marketing department that was frustrated with its traditional, top-down training. The employees felt the courses were generic and disconnected from their daily work. Leadership was skeptical of new AI tools, so the team was falling behind.

Instead of rolling out a massive, expensive training program, we suggested a different approach. We designated one small, cross-functional team and gave them a challenge: "Here is a new AI tool. You have thirty days to experiment with it on one small workflow. Your only mandate is to document what you learn, both the successes and the failures."

The result was a breakthrough. The team discovered the tool wasn't good for the task they were initially given. But in the process, they found an entirely new way to use it to automate a different, more tedious task that no one had even considered. Their thirty days of "failure" led to a discovery that saved hundreds of hours a year, freed them up for more creative work, and ultimately became a new best practice for the entire department. More importantly, they built a new confidence in their ability to solve problems and a palpable excitement around the new technology.

What matters most is building a training environment that looks forward, adapts to context, connects to purpose, includes leadership, and offers the right mix of guidance and freedom. When you get those ingredients right, your people don't just learn; they transform.

Embedding Learning in the Flow of Work

One of the most common misconceptions I hear is that learning is a box to check, a course to complete, a credential to collect, or a session to attend. But in environments where AI is rapidly reshaping how work gets done, that model breaks down almost immediately. The half-life of technical skills is shrinking, new tools are emerging weekly, and yesterday's knowledge may already be obsolete tomorrow. The only way to keep pace is to build a workplace where learning doesn't happen outside the job; it's woven into the job itself.

The only way to keep pace is to build a workplace where learning doesn't happen outside the job; it's woven into the job itself.

This means making learning a continuous, embedded, and reflexive part of how work happens. In the most successful transformation environments I've seen, teams learn as fast as they deliver. They treat experimentation as part of execution. When something doesn't go as planned, the focus isn't on blame but on insight. The misstep becomes a contribution, because now the team knows something they didn't know before.

That mindset starts with creating space for what I call *digital curiosity*. This isn't just a trait reserved for IT or data science. It has to show up in every function. Finance teams need to ask how automation could reduce error rates. Operations teams should explore how predictive analytics could optimize scheduling. Marketers need to test how generative tools can accelerate campaign development. Curiosity doesn't mean you always have the right answer. It means you're willing to ask the right questions, then follow where they lead.

Embedding learning also means moving away from feedback that's driven by hierarchy or gut feel. Too often, the loudest voice in the room wins the day, even when it's disconnected from the reality of the work. Data changes that. When you track how people use new tools, how they collaborate across functions, or how quickly they adapt to changes, you start to build a learning loop that's rooted in evidence instead of opinion.

This is where AI becomes not just a tool for work but a partner in learning. Take the example of digital twins—virtual models of real systems that allow teams to experiment in safe environments. In a manufacturing setting, a team might simulate production changes to test how small adjustments affect yield. That same logic applies to knowledge work. You can test new processes in a sandbox, tweak data inputs, and analyze results before rolling out changes across the board. The result is faster insight, fewer unintended consequences, and a more confident approach to change.

The teams that do this well build internal knowledge bases in parallel. I've seen teams use screen recordings of colleagues performing key tasks, annotate those clips with commentary, and tag them to relevant documentation. This goes beyond knowledge capture to knowledge transfer. And because it's built by people doing the work, it's far more accessible and relevant than the average training deck.

What emerges is a shared language of learning. The veteran in customer success records a walkthrough of how she handles a tricky escalation. The new hire in operations rewrites a process doc after discovering a better sequence. A product manager tags a lesson learned in the latest sprint review so that future teams don't repeat the same misstep. None of these are formal training moments. But they're all moments of embedded learning. And over time, they form a learning system that's distributed, adaptive, and durable.

This shift also requires us to celebrate a different kind of excellence. Historically, we've rewarded the person who knew the most or made the fewest mistakes. But in a world of rapid change, those aren't the most valuable traits. The more valuable traits are learning quickly, unlearning when necessary, and bringing others along in the process. The employee who documents their process so others can improve it, even if it's still imperfect, is doing more for the team than the one who keeps knowledge close and rarely stumbles.

The employee who documents their process so others can improve it, even if it's still imperfect, is doing more for the team than the one who keeps knowledge close and rarely stumbles.

The organizations that thrive in this era will be the ones that understand this distinction. They will use AI not just to optimize tasks but to surface insights, test scenarios, and guide development in real time. And they will treat learning as a durable habit, one that turns every challenge into an opportunity to grow.

Redefining Performance for the AI Era

If you walk into most organizations today and ask about performance management, you'll probably hear some version of the same thing: a backward-looking review process, often conducted once or twice a year, focused on what someone did, how well they did it, and whether that aligned with a predefined set of goals. On the surface, that may sound logical. But in a world being reshaped by AI and rapid digital transformation, this approach is not only outdated; it's counterproductive.

The old model was built for stability. It rewarded predictability, consistency, and adherence to plans. But transformation work demands something different. Skills such as agility, curiosity, collaboration, and a willingness to evolve. That's why performance in the AI era can't be measured solely by static metrics or outcomes. It has to reflect how people learn, adapt, and contribute in motion.

Performance in the AI era can't be measured solely by static metrics or outcomes. It has to reflect how people learn, adapt, and contribute in motion.

This is where AI becomes a powerful partner. When used thoughtfully, AI can surface signals of performance that traditional reviews miss entirely. Instead of looking only at end results, it can highlight patterns of behavior such as how someone engages with learning content, how they show up in collaborative workflows, how frequently they contribute to cross-functional problem-solving, or how they incorporate feedback into their work. These signals are subtle but revealing, painting a picture of what someone accomplished, how they got there, and how equipped they are for what's next.

One of the clearest shifts we're seeing is a move from output-based performance to contribution-based performance. Instead of just asking, Did this person hit their target? we start asking, What kind of momentum did they create? Did they help the team move faster? Did they improve a process? Did they elevate others around them? AI can track participation in real time, everything from document edits to project commitments to meeting input, and when connected to thoughtful analysis, it can reveal the shape of someone's contribution far more completely than a manager's memory of the last quarter.

In this technological revolution, one could argue that the half-life of specific skills is shrinking rapidly. Which means that the demand for meta-skills—learning agility, adaptation, and collaboration, the kind of contribution-based skills that drive innovation and enable possibility—is only going to compound over time. The organizations that will experience transformation or continue to thrive are those that build performance development into their DNA, treating every project, every challenge, and every technological advancement as an opportunity to grow collective capability. Because this approach not only benefits the organization but also the employees—everybody wins. Careers advance, capability deepens, and the business gains increasingly skilled contributors.

When performance is framed as a developmental journey rather than a pass/fail evaluation, it invites a different kind of engagement. People stop worrying about getting dinged for what they didn't do and start focusing on what they're learning, how they're growing, and where they can stretch next. The review becomes a conversation about direction, not just destination.

When employees genuinely feel and understand this from their leadership, a collective resiliency and accountability forms. People are more invested in their success on both an individual and team level because you, as their leader, are investing more in their success—transforming what's historically been mindless into a mindful, consistent practice. This commitment from the top is like a pebble in a still pond, creating a ripple effect as your teams further reinforce your transformation strategy by reflecting back the same commitment.

Of course, for this to work, the system must be transparent and fair. Employees need to know what signals are being measured, how those signals connect to performance insights, and what context is being considered. If someone experimented with a new tool and struggled initially but made meaningful progress over time, the system should capture that growth. If a person took the lead on mentoring others or contributing to shared documentation, that should be visible and valued. Otherwise, we risk replacing one narrow system with another.

That's why it's so important to shift from viewing performance development as a scorecard to seeing it as a compass. The goal isn't to judge where someone has been; it's to help them orient toward where they can go. AI makes that compass sharper. In a consistent, ongoing process, AI can help spot emerging strengths, surface hidden contributors, and identify the kind of support different people need to thrive. It can also highlight patterns of collaboration or disengagement that would otherwise remain invisible until it was too late to intervene.

And when these insights are paired with real human conversations, they gain richer context. Managers can coach more effectively, spot burnout sooner, and help employees connect their day-to-day work to a broader sense of purpose.

This kind of performance system builds capability. It encourages experimentation, rewards initiative, and strengthens the feedback loops that make teams more adaptive.

Discovering Hidden Potential Through AI Insight

Most organizations assume they know who their top performers are. They rely on formal titles, past reviews, or visible project success. But when you start digging into the data and really examine how work gets done, where influence lives, and how people engage with new challenges, what you often find is surprising. The people driving progress aren't always the ones in the spotlight. They're often buried in customer support queues, in code comments, or behind meeting invites, where they're quietly solving the next big problem. AI gives us a chance to see them.

Whether you're adopting new analytics capabilities or enhancing existing performance management systems, AI can surface contributors who might otherwise be overlooked by analyzing patterns in communication, collaboration, and learning behavior. These are the "hidden gems"—people who demonstrate high learning agility, share knowledge without being asked, and raise their hands to try new tools or troubleshoot emerging problems. They may not check every box on a traditional leadership rubric, but they are leading in the ways that matter now.

One of the most meaningful signals AI can capture is how someone responds to change. In a fast-moving world, adaptability is as important as expertise. Are they taking initiative in learning new systems? Are they actively contributing to evolving processes? Do they lean into ambiguity or step back from it? These are qualities that often go unnoticed in static performance reviews. But in the continuous flow of real work, they show up again and again. And now, with the right data inputs, we can begin to track and elevate them.

In a fast-moving world, adaptability is as important as expertise.

AI also helps us identify informal leaders, those who influence others not through title but through trust. It could be the developer whose pull requests are consistently studied by others. The analyst whose training videos get shared across teams. The project manager who creates clarity during chaos. These signals live in our systems. AI can see them, trace the network effects, and bring to light contributions that are often too subtle for the naked eye.

But visibility is only part of the equation. The other half is fairness. Because as powerful as AI is, it can still mirror the biases of the data it learns from or the assumptions baked into its design. If it's only trained to recognize certain kinds of outputs, it may miss value created in other forms. If it reflects past performance patterns rooted in inequity, it may reinforce the very gaps we're trying to close.

That's why explainability matters. Every AI-driven insight about potential should be traceable. What signals were analyzed? What weight was given to different behaviors or data sources? How might someone review, question, or refine the result? Transparency isn't a nice-to-have here; it's foundational. Without it, we risk replacing old blind spots with new ones, just wearing fancier lenses.

And just as importantly, AI should never operate alone. Data without judgment is noise. Human insight provides the context, empathy, and lived experience that makes sense of what the system sees. The goal isn't to automate talent decisions; it's to augment them. Think of AI as a copilot. It might notice something you missed, offer a new angle, or challenge an assumption. But the final decision remains a human responsibility.

Think of AI as a copilot. It might notice something you missed, offer a new angle, or challenge an assumption. But the final decision remains a human responsibility.

Of course, all of this rests on a foundation of trust. If employees believe AI is being used to rank, sort, or punish, they'll disengage. But if it's framed and experienced as a tool for growth, for surfacing opportunities, matching them to development paths, and helping them navigate their careers with more clarity, then it becomes empowering. The key is protecting data privacy, minimizing unnecessary exposure, and being ruthlessly transparent about what's collected, why it's used, and how it will benefit the person being assessed.

Done well, this kind of insight can be transformational. It doesn't just help organizations make better decisions. It helps individuals see a future for themselves they may not have considered. It says: You have value here, even if it hasn't been visible yet.

That's the real promise of AI in talent discovery. Not a faster way to rank resumes but a more human way to reveal and nurture the full spectrum of talent already inside the business.

FIVE STEPS TO TAKE NOW

Equipping your workforce for the age of AI means rewiring how learning happens across the organization by embedding curiosity into the culture, making space for experimentation, and using technology as a partner in growth, not just for automation.

The five steps below are designed to spark that shift. They're grounded in real-world practice and built to be actionable whether you lead a small team or a global enterprise.

Step 1: Embed Learning in the Flow of Work

Pick one high-value workflow—customer support tickets, financial reporting, product QA—and look for where real-time learning could live inside it.

Ask:

- Where do people pause to seek help?
- What questions come up again and again?
- Could AI surface guidance at that moment?

Now identify one team member doing the work well, and document their process. Turn it into a short video, annotated standard operating procedure, or interactive demo others can learn from, then build it into the workflow. Learning doesn't need to be a course. It can be a moment, a pattern, or a nudge, delivered when and where it's needed most.

Step 2: Run a "Teach-and-Learn" Session

Schedule a forty-five-minute session where one team shares what they've learned using a new digital tool or method.

Format:

- Ten minutes: What problem were we trying to solve?
- Ten minutes: What did we try, and what surprised us?
- Ten minutes: What didn't work, and why?
- Fifteen minutes: Open Q&A

Make this informal, inclusive, and regular. The goal is shared insight. You'll be amazed how quickly peer-led learning spreads when you make it visible, safe, and valuable.

Step 3: Launch a "Curiosity Sprint"

Block two hours this week for each team to explore one AI tool or process innovation outside their usual responsibilities. Encourage them to ask:

- How could this make our work better, faster, or smarter?
- Where might this go wrong, and how would we course-correct?
- What could we try right now, in low-risk ways?

Leaders should participate, too, but as fellow learners. Curiosity is contagious when modeled from the top.

Step 4: Redefine What Great Performance Looks Like

Bring your leadership team together and ask a provocative question: What are we rewarding today, and does it match the behavior we need for tomorrow?

If learning agility, collaboration, and experimentation matter, they should show up in how performance is assessed and celebrated. Look at how growth is measured today. If it's all backward-looking metrics and output volume, start introducing signals like contribution quality, knowledge-sharing, and engagement with new tools. Small shifts here can send powerful signals.

Step 5: Use AI to Surface Hidden Potential

Choose one function, such as customer support or operations, and partner with HR or your data team to analyze workflow contributions, communication patterns, and learning activity.

Look for:

- Who's consistently experimenting or solving novel problems
- Who's mentoring others without a formal title
- Who's using learning resources in unexpected but high-leverage ways

Use these insights to spark new conversations about talent development. You may discover emerging leaders or overlooked experts simply by looking through a new lens.

PART III

POWERING UP FOR TRANSFORMATION

CHAPTER FIVE

BUILDING A CULTURE OF INNOVATION

If everything seems under control, you're not going fast enough.

—MARIO ANDRETTI

Your Mission Possible Blueprint: Innovation culture beats innovation labs every time. This chapter shows you how to embed experimentation, learning, and adaptation into your organization's DNA. You'll walk away with five specific ways to foster the mindset that turns disruption into opportunity.

WHEN MOST LEADERS hear the word *innovation*, their minds jump to the obvious: launching new products, adopting flashy technology, or standing up an internal team tasked with dreaming up the next big idea. But after decades of watching what actually drives durable growth across industries, I've come to believe that this definition is far too narrow ... and far too fragile. Innovation isn't a job title, a department, or a short-term campaign. It's an operating system. And like any good operating system, it needs to run quietly, reliably, and consistently in the background of everything your organization does.

Innovation isn't a job title, a department, or a short-term campaign. It's an operating system.

This becomes especially clear in the era we're living in now, one when data, AI, and intelligent technologies are fundamentally reshaping what's possible. And those technologies that enable innovation today will themselves evolve rapidly. Build a culture of innovation, not to chase the shiny new thing but to innovate your processes and operations. Making innovation your operating system requires not just adapting to change but anticipating it, learning from it, and using each advancement as a springboard for the next breakthrough. But unlocking that potential doesn't start with a procurement decision or a software rollout. It starts with how your organization thinks. The mindset behind the work. The way decisions get made, and by whom. The posture your teams take toward uncertainty, and the appetite they have for discovering what's next.

Every leader I know is under pressure to deliver results such as efficiency gains and reliable forecasts. That's the job. But the mistake I see too often is assuming that innovation is something you pursue *after* those boxes are checked. It gets relegated to the margins, an optional initiative when there's time or budget. That approach might feel comfortable, but it's a trap. In reality, the most resilient companies bake innovation into the core of how they operate.

That shift starts with reframing the role of leadership itself. Managing for incremental improvement might keep things moving in the short term, but it won't prepare your business for the next curve. Building a true innovation culture demands that leaders challenge their own default patterns, especially the ones that worked in the past. It means creating space to ask different questions, to pause on what's familiar, and to resist the gravitational pull of precedent.

In practice, this also means recognizing where innovation lives. It's easy to assume it only shows up in the R&D lab, the marketing team, or the engineering org. But I've seen some of the most transformative ideas come from process teams buried in the middle of the org chart, or frontline employees who have direct line of sight into the customer's real experience. Real innovation doesn't discriminate. It shows up wherever people are empowered to rethink, redesign, and reimagine how value gets created and delivered.

Real innovation doesn't discriminate. It shows up wherever people are empowered to rethink, redesign, and reimagine how value gets created and delivered.

That includes product, of course, but also service models, workflows, partner strategies, data usage, and internal systems. I've worked with logistics companies that reinvented how goods were tracked, not what was shipped. I've seen insurance firms drive massive growth not by changing policies but by transforming the claims process to reduce stress and uncertainty for customers. In every case, the catalyst wasn't a bolt of inspiration. It was a deliberate shift in the way the organization operated and thought.

When innovation becomes embedded in the operating system, a few things change. Teams stop waiting for permission to try something new. Leaders stop relying solely on legacy metrics to guide decisions.

Experimentation gets normalized. And perhaps most importantly, curiosity becomes contagious.

That's the work. Not glamorized, loud, or always headline-worthy. And the good news is, it's not out of reach. You don't need to overhaul your entire organization overnight. You just need to commit to making innovation part of how you operate every day.

In the early days of AWS, we built innovation into our operating system. We had a principle we called "The Builder's Oath." It was simple: Every team, no matter how small, had the autonomy to launch an experiment, fail fast, and iterate.

I remember a time when our retail website was struggling with a bottleneck during a major holiday sale. A small engineering team—not a top-down executive team—saw the problem and, without asking for permission, built a new microservice to solve it. This wasn't in their mandate. It wasn't on the road map. They simply saw a problem, built a solution, and deployed it. The entire fix took just forty-eight hours and not only saved the day but fundamentally changed how we thought about deployment.

This wasn't a glamorous, headline-worthy moment. It was a cultural shift that became embedded in our day-to-day operations. It's what allowed us to stop relying on legacy metrics and start rewarding curiosity. And that is the work that leads to real, lasting transformation.

The Day One Mindset, Amplified

At Amazon, we had a phrase that guided almost everything: *It's still day one*. It was a reminder that complacency is the beginning of decline. The businesses that endure aren't the ones that rest on past success but the ones that show up every day with the urgency, curiosity, and energy of a startup. That mindset is even more critical now, in a world shaped by intelligent technology.

The businesses that endure aren't the ones that rest on past success but the ones that show up every day with the urgency, curiosity, and energy of a startup.

What does day one look like when AI and data are embedded in every decision and workflow? It might look like taking nothing for granted, or like using data not just to report the past but to anticipate what's next. It can look like being willing to challenge deeply held assumptions about how your business creates value in the first place.

When I talk with leadership teams about innovation, the first shift I ask them to make is this: Start every initiative by working backward. Begin with the ideal customer or employee experience you want to create. Define it clearly. Describe it in human terms. What does seamless look like? What does delight feel like? What friction needs to disappear?

Once you've got that picture, capture it in writing, like a press release. Describe the result as if it's already happened. What's the headline? What problem did you solve? What changed for the customer? What tangible impact did it have on the business? This is a practice we used frequently at Amazon, and I still recommend it to teams navigating AI initiatives today.

The exercise may feel awkward at first, especially if you're wired to jump straight into execution. But there's a reason it works. Writing that press release forces clarity. It strips away the buzzwords and makes you confront the actual value you intend to deliver while aligning teams on what matters, exposing gaps in thinking long before you've spent time or money building the wrong thing.

In the age of intelligent technology, this kind of discipline is essential. AI and other emerging technologies give us more power than ever to automate, analyze, and optimize. But if you don't anchor those efforts in a clear, desired outcome, you risk spinning up initiatives that look impressive on the surface and deliver very little in the end. I've seen teams launch machine learning pilots with beautiful models and no business impact. I've seen chatbots rolled out before the customer pain point was fully understood. Those companies missed the memo: Tech alone won't save you.

That's why day one thinking has to extend beyond product teams. It belongs in every corner of the business. Finance. HR. Sales. Operations. Wherever decisions are being made about how people work, how customers engage, or how the business evolves. Intelligent technology is a horizontal layer across everything. Which means the discipline of working backward has to be just as widespread.

Innovation Starts with the Customer (and the Employee)

In every transformation effort, I come back to two questions: What's making it hard for each individual ME—your customer—to get what they want the first time they try? And what's making it hard for each employee ME to deliver that seamlessly?

Most organizations can't answer with clarity. They point to broken processes or outdated tools. Some cite legacy systems or compliance constraints. But in my experience, those are just surface-level symptoms. The real problem is more fundamental: a lack of visibility into where the friction really lives and, most importantly, why it exists.

The work isn't in fixing the symptoms. It's in finding and eliminating that core friction. That's the real work of a leader.

When you're serious about building a culture of innovation, your first instinct has to shift from building new features to uncovering the unmet needs of MEx. That starts with listening, not building. Listen with intent, through data, and with humility. You have to see what the customer sees, feel what they feel, and experience every interaction as if you were the one on the receiving end.

When you're serious about building a culture of innovation, your first instinct has to shift from building new features to uncovering the unmet needs of MEx.

That's what customer obsession really means. It's not just having a few nice personas taped to the whiteboard; it's doing the hard work of analyzing behavior, identifying drop-offs, and studying feedback loops in detail. Intelligent technologies now give us the ability to surface these friction points at scale, often in ways traditional survey data never could. From sentiment analysis of support interactions to heatmaps of user flows through digital experiences, the signals are there. The challenge is being willing to look.

Should you accept that challenge, you'll often find that the biggest blockers aren't technical, they're emotional: confusion, frustration, uncertainty. You can build the most sophisticated workflow in the world, but if the customer doesn't trust or doesn't understand it, you've already lost. AI-powered analytics can help detect those invisible signals: the phrases customers use when they hesitate, the points at which they abandon your process, the questions they repeat even after you think you've answered them. These are your opportunity zones. And this is where innovation begins.

But here's the part most organizations miss: The same rigor needs to be applied to your employee experience. Innovation goes beyond the marketplace to how work gets done inside your walls. Your people are navigating your systems every day. They are the ones closest to your processes, your policies, your customers. If they're spending half their time working around the tools you've given them, or if the internal friction is so high that nothing moves without escalation, you don't have a technology problem; you have a trust problem.

Working backward from the ideal employee experience is just as important as doing so for the customer. Ask: What does seamless look like for the frontline manager trying to serve a client? What does clarity look like for the team member navigating a policy change? What does empowerment feel like for someone trying to experiment or speak up with an idea?

The good news is you don't have to guess. The data is there, if you're willing to use it. Behavioral analytics can show where processes break. Employee sentiment tools can surface where confidence is low or frustration is building. Look at how many clicks it takes to complete a task. Watch where information gets lost between systems. Track how many times employees say, "I just figured out a workaround."

Every one of those signals is the start of an innovation opportunity. Not because it's shiny or disruptive, but because it removes friction and unlocks potential.

When you combine these two lenses, customer *and* employee, you create a virtuous cycle. As you make life easier for your people, they serve your customers better. As your customers respond, your teams become more engaged. And all of it is powered by a deep, relentless commitment to finding and solving the invisible blockers that most companies overlook.

Innovation isn't a onetime event; it begins with your next meeting. The real breakthrough will come once you stop trying to find a solution and start asking the right questions that challenge your assumptions and unlock new ways of thinking.

Don't start with a long-term road map. Start with the people you serve. Always ask yourself: What would make this simpler, faster, or more meaningful for the MEx?

Imagine a room full of your smartest leaders. Now, ask them to set aside everything they know about your current process. Ask them: What would this look like if we started from scratch? What would delight, not just satisfy, the people we serve?

These questions are powerful because they cost nothing to ask, but they change everything. In my experience, this exercise forces teams to think beyond incremental improvements and focus on genuine human problems. It's not about finding a magic bullet; it's about building a culture where curiosity becomes contagious and your people are empowered to deliver breakthroughs every day.

The benefits of this mindset extend beyond your customers to your employees, too. When you empower your teams to ask these questions and take ownership of a problem, a few things happen. Most importantly, you build engagement and loyalty. Employees feel valued when they are asked to solve real problems, not just follow a rigid process. In empowering them, you uncover new skills. Giving people the freedom to experiment and fail fast allows them to discover new talents and passions that would otherwise be hidden. When you add in a culture of ownership—when employees see that their ideas can lead to real breakthroughs—everyone becomes more invested in the success of the business.

This is the key to building a resilient and transformative culture. The same mindset that delights customers is what will also empower your people to do their best work.

Small Teams, Big Leverage

One of the most counterintuitive truths in the age of intelligent technology is this: Scale doesn't begin with size. It begins with a small team of people who are clear on the problem they're trying to solve, and who have the space, autonomy, and tools to solve it.

Scale doesn't begin with size. It begins with a small team of people who are clear on the problem they're trying to solve, and who have the space, autonomy, and tools to solve it.

At AWS, we used to talk about "two-pizza" teams. Small teams force clarity and surface gaps in understanding quickly. They make it easier to course-correct without losing momentum. And when they're given direct access to data, intelligent tools, and the freedom to iterate, they can drive change faster than any committee ever will.

But autonomy alone isn't enough. These teams need structure around that freedom, not to mention a defined outcome to work toward. They need rapid feedback loops and access to relevant data. They need clear decision rights and the psychological safety to move without fear of failure. Most importantly, they need leaders willing to protect their space.

When you empower team members like that, amazing things happen. They start to surface insights the larger organization hasn't been able to see, uncovering patterns, gaps, and dependencies that often remain hidden when innovation is left to slide decks and strategy sessions. And because they're closer to the customer or employee pain point they're solving, their solutions are often more grounded, more usable, and more impactful than anything dreamed up from a distance.

These teams thrive when the mandate is tied to a specific outcome: Reduce customer churn by 10 percent, halve onboarding time, eliminate manual handoffs in a high-friction workflow. The specificity sharpens their decisions and creates a shared understanding of what success looks like.

Give these teams access to your AI tooling, your analytics platforms, and your real-time feedback channels. Let them test ideas, not just theorize. Let them learn what works, what breaks, and what needs to evolve. Then share what they learn, including what didn't work. The most valuable outcome of a small team experiment isn't always the solution they build; it's the insight they uncover that shapes what the rest of the organization should do next.

Can you learn something meaningful, quickly, that helps inform where to invest next? Can you move from insight to action without getting stuck in endless validation cycles? And when something doesn't work, can you extract the anti-patterns and codify the lessons? If the answer is yes, then you're on your way to building a culture in which innovation is constant, not episodic. And you're doing it in a way that scales.

Make Failure Safe and Learning Visible

There's a strange paradox in most organizations. Leaders talk about the importance of innovation, agility, and experimentation. But when something doesn't go as planned—when a prototype flops or a data model underperforms—the reflex is still to blame, minimize, or quietly shelve it. And so, despite good intentions, the organization stays cautious. Risk-averse. Optimized for predictability, not progress.

That's a cultural bug, not a feature. And if you want innovation to take root, you have to fix it at the source.

The first step is rethinking what failure actually is. In a culture of innovation, failure isn't a breakdown. It's a data point, a boundary test. It's the part of the exploration cycle that tells you what won't work so you can more quickly figure out what will. When teams know they can run bounded experiments without getting punished for every misstep, they become smarter, not reckless. And over time, they become more confident in their ability to navigate the unknown.

When teams know they can run bounded experiments without getting punished for every misstep, they become smarter, not reckless.

What I've seen in the best innovation environments is a deliberate shift from perfection to progress. Leaders explicitly say: We're not measuring success by how few mistakes we make. We're measuring how quickly we learn. Learning velocity becomes the new gold standard. How fast did we move from assumption to insight? How many testable ideas did we explore this quarter? What patterns, positive and negative, did we uncover? And how are we sharing those learnings across the organization?

This is where anti-patterns come in. Too often, teams hide what didn't work because they're worried it'll be used against them. But those "failures" are actually some of the most valuable assets you have. When shared openly and constructively, they prevent duplication of mistakes and sharpen decision-making across functions. And they normalize a growth mindset that's rooted in data, not ego.

In the early days of AWS, we deliberately shifted our mindset from perfection to progress. We weren't measured by how few mistakes we made; we were measured by how quickly we learned. This wasn't just a slogan; it was embedded in our operating system.

I remember a time when our retail business wanted to build a new payment feature. The traditional approach would have been a long, multimonth project with endless meetings and a big, onetime launch. Instead, we broke it into small, testable pieces. A team was given permission to launch a simple, low-risk test to just 1 percent of our customers. The first version failed, the second had a major bug, but the third one clicked.

The genius of this approach was that we measured learning velocity. Every failure was a data point. The ME of each developer felt empowered to take a chance, and the ME of the customer gave us real-time feedback. We learned more in a single quarter of rapid, small-scale experiments than we would have in a year of traditional development. This allowed us to quickly pivot, find the right solution, and scale it to millions of customers. We learned that the real value isn't in getting it right the first time; it's in building a culture in which getting it right eventually is a foregone conclusion because you've created a learning machine.

At AWS, and in many companies I've advised since, we implemented a simple but powerful practice: debriefs after every experiment, regardless of outcome. What hypothesis were we testing? What did the data show? What surprised us? What would we try differently next time? These debriefs were designed to build collective intelligence while making sure the insights didn't stay siloed in a single team or project.

To make this work at scale, teams need permission, but they also need structure. This is where metrics such as learnings per dollar come into play. If you're going to fund intelligent technology initiatives—AI pilots, data-driven workflow improvements, predictive models—you want to know you're not just burning money. But rather than obsessing over immediate ROI, focus on the insight return: What did we learn per unit of investment? How did this inform our road map, our customer experience, or our operational model?

This approach encourages teams to experiment deliberately, not randomly. You set boundaries: time, scope, data parameters. You tie each effort to a defined outcome, ideally anchored in a customer or employee friction point. And you make the results, successes *and* failures, available to others trying to solve adjacent problems.

That visibility is critical. Without it, every team is flying blind, reinventing the same wheel or stepping into the same potholes. With it, your organization develops a shared muscle for rapid discovery and data-informed iteration. And over time, the signal-to-noise ratio improves. You stop chasing ideas that sound good and start investing in ideas that prove themselves quickly.

If you want speed, insight, and strategic clarity in this new era, make failure safe.

Rewarding Discovery, Not Just Delivery

If you're serious about building a culture of innovation, you can't stop at inspiration. You have to take a hard look at what the organization *actually rewards*. Because in practice, people will follow the compensation. If bonuses and promotions are tied solely to quarterly performance and operating margin, then don't be surprised when teams avoid experimentation and stick to what's predictable. The reward system becomes the operating system, and in many cases, it's directly at odds with the behaviors that innovation demands.

To truly shift the organization toward long-term value creation, incentives must reflect a new set of priorities. That's done by rewarding discovery, not just delivery. Recognize validated learning, even if the experiment didn't yield an immediate revenue bump. Build incentives around collaboration across silos, especially when solving complex, cross-functional problems. The moment your teams realize that uncovering strategic options for the future is just as valuable, if not more so, than maximizing the next quarter, that's when innovation starts to get real traction.

To truly shift the organization toward long-term value creation, incentives must reflect a new set of priorities. That's done by rewarding discovery, not just delivery.

I've seen this shift play out at scale. At Amazon, for example, Jeff Bezos made long-term thinking a bedrock principle. That didn't mean being aloof to short-term performance, but it did mean placing calculated bets that might not pay off for years. AWS is the canonical example because it took time to mature. And once it did, it redefined the industry. Those investments were based on evidence of customer pull and emerging opportunity, not immediate financial return. And incentives were structured to support that journey of strategic discovery, not to punish it.

Other companies are starting to follow suit now. I've worked with leaders who tie a percentage of their long-term compensation to the number of validated insights generated each quarter or the breadth of strategic options explored, essentially measuring learning velocity as a proxy for future value creation. That kind of structure reinforces the idea that innovation isn't a side project; it's a deliberate, disciplined pursuit that's worth being compensated for. It encourages people to be intellectually honest and curious, to run thoughtful experiments, and to extract meaningful learnings even when things don't go to plan.

This shift also applies to teams across the org. One practice I've found powerful is tying innovation KPIs to cross-functional outcomes. When two teams are stuck in their own lanes, it's easy to play the blame game. But if you give them a shared customer problem to solve and a joint bonus tied to the outcome, suddenly everything changes. Marketing and logistics start sharing data. And more often than not, they come back with solutions that neither team could've come up with on their own.

But if you don't make this shift, you fall into the trap of *innovation theater*. That's when everyone talks about being innovative, there are brainstorming sessions with sticky notes on whiteboards, and decks get built that say all the right words. But nothing actually changes. No value gets delivered. No processes are improved. No customers are delighted. I've seen it too often: A well-packaged presentation earns a bonus, but the work stops there. And leadership walks away with the illusion that progress is being made.

To counter this, reward not just the idea but the *execution*. Reward the team that tested a hypothesis, collected the data, realized it didn't work, and used that learning to refine the next iteration. Celebrate the anti-patterns, the experiments that revealed what *not* to do. When those are made visible and rewarded, you accelerate collective intelligence across the organization. And you send a powerful signal that learning is the metric that matters.

The flip side is also important: Punishing failure, even unintentionally, is a cultural cancer. The moment someone gets sidelined or shamed for an experiment that didn't pan out, the learning stops. Risk tolerance vanishes. And what you're left with is a workforce that optimizes for safety instead of growth. This is especially damaging when financial ROI becomes the sole metric of success. Yes, ROI matters. But in the early stages of exploring something new, impact may not show up as dollars. It may show up as insight. And that insight could unlock a future breakthrough.

Make Learning a Shared Habit

If you want innovation to last, it can't be a sprint. It has to be a rhythm.

Most companies wait until there's a crisis to rethink how they operate. The business starts lagging, a competitor pulls ahead, a new technology arrives, and suddenly, there's a flurry of initiatives and executive offsites designed to "ignite transformation." But by then, the window to lead may already be closing. Reinvention shouldn't be a reflex to disruption. It should be a reflex, *period*.

> *Reinvention shouldn't be a reflex to disruption.*
> *It should be a reflex*, period.

That's why the most future-ready organizations don't treat innovation as a onetime event. They build systems into their cultures to make learning visible, regular, and shared. These systems don't have to be flashy, just consistent.

One of the most effective habits I've seen is the use of biweekly innovation reviews. These are working sessions where teams present what they've tested, what the data showed, what they learned, and what they're doing next. In these sessions, we don't reward polish. We reward insight. And we do it out loud, so the entire room benefits from the signal.

Another practice I've found invaluable is implementing formal correction-of-error (COE) documents. When something doesn't work, such as an AI model misfiring or a pilot falling short, we don't hide it, we *analyze* it. These COEs focus on root cause, what we didn't anticipate, what the data showed, and how we're adjusting. Then we make them available to other teams. That way, one failure becomes a thousand people's insight.

And then there's storytelling. Innovation needs its own narrative channels. Internal newsletters, Slack updates, short dispatches from the edge, whatever format fits your culture, find a way to surface the cool, the strange, and the instructive. Highlight the three-person team that built a prototype over a weekend. Share how a failed segmentation experiment revealed a hidden customer segment. Spotlight the anti-pattern that saved someone else from running in circles. What you are doing is reinforcing a mindset. A mindset that every team has a voice and the pursuit of better is worth paying attention to.

Hackathons are another powerful ritual, especially when you focus them on real business problems. These are cross-functional sprints where teams build scrappy prototypes to address internal inefficiencies or customer pain points. Done well, they not only produce useful tools; they uncover new ideas, build relationships across silos, and energize the culture. And because they're time-boxed, they force clarity and action.

But none of this matters if it happens in isolation. The real shift comes when learning becomes a *shared* habit. That's what separates pockets of innovation from a true reinvention culture. Leaders have to model it. Teams have to expect it. And the organization has to value it out loud.

Think of innovation like a muscle. If you only train it during emergencies, it won't be ready when you need it most. But if you exercise it regularly, with small experiments, deliberate rituals, and visible reflection, it becomes second nature.

The goal isn't to predict every future wave of technological change. The goal is to build an organization that can surf whatever wave comes next. You can't do that just by buying a perfect, premade surfboard. You do it by empowering every ME—every customer and every employee—with the confidence, curiosity, and collective capability to turn disruption into opportunity. The strength of the wave is irrelevant if you have an organization of world-class surfers. Your job as a leader isn't to predict the future. It's to build the team that can own it.

The goal isn't to predict every future wave of technological change. The goal is to build an organization that can surf whatever wave comes next.

FIVE STEPS TO TAKE NOW

Building a culture of innovation begins with behavior change from the top down and the edges in. These are deliberate choices to operate differently, to learn in public, and to build long-term advantage in a world that punishes stagnation. If you're ready to shift from slogans to substance, here are five practical places to begin:

1. Institutionalize Working Backward Thinking

Embed the practice of starting every initiative, especially those involving AI and intelligent technology, with a clear articulation of the customer or employee outcome you aim to achieve. Begin with a draft "press release" that defines success from their perspective. What benefit are you delivering? How will it feel, look, and function? This forces clarity before investment and shifts teams out of feature-building mode and into problem-solving mode.

2. Create a Two-Pizza Team with Real Authority

Identify a strategic problem worth solving, and form a small, cross-functional team, no bigger than two pizzas could feed, to tackle it. Give them direct access to data, clear decision rights, and a limited but protected budget. Insulate them from day-to-day firefighting and hold them accountable to learning velocity and outcomes, not perfection. Innovation needs space to breathe, not layers of approvals to suffocate under.

3. Redesign Incentives Around Discovery, Not Delivery

Update compensation and performance systems to reflect the value of learning. Reward validated insights, customer experimentation, and team-driven collaboration. Shift incentives away from output volume and toward outcome clarity. If someone ran an experiment that disproved a faulty assumption and saved the company from a misfire, that's worth recognizing, not burying. Innovation grows where discovery is celebrated.

4. Establish Learning Rituals That Stick

Block time for learning reviews at every level of the business. Make space for COE, cross-functional show-and-tells, and small-stage demo days. Launch an internal innovation newsletter or dispatch channel where teams share breakthroughs and lessons, including the ideas that didn't land. What matters is not just the success rate but how fast your organization learns and how broadly those learnings are shared.

5. Reclaim Executive Time for Thinking, Not Just Reacting

If you're in a leadership role, set aside unmovable time each week to think strategically, not reactively. Use that time to explore intelligent tech trends, review what experiments are unfolding, and reflect on the organizational friction you may be unconsciously reinforcing. Schedule time with customers and frontline employees. Stay close to the edge, where unmet needs live. The future doesn't wait, and your job isn't to manage the present; it's to invent what comes next.

CHAPTER SIX

DEMYSTIFYING EMERGING TECHNOLOGIES

*Technology overreacts in the short run and underperforms
in the long run—unless you build for what's coming.*

—ADAPTED FROM AMARA'S LAW

Your Mission Possible Blueprint: Technology choices made today determine competitive position tomorrow. This chapter cuts through the hype to show you how to evaluate and implement emerging technologies strategically. You'll complete this with five practical approaches to technology decision-making that create lasting advantage.

IN THE EARLY days of AWS, we were working with ideas that felt almost intangible. We were inventing something from what felt like thin air, yet the goal was clear: Build infrastructure that functioned like a utility. Not like cable, which people accept reluctantly, but like electricity or water—dependable, seamless, and always available. The aspiration was simple to articulate but complex to engineer. To deliver on that promise, we had to build not just for performance but for trust.

That meant shifting focus from the visible to the invisible. Customers interact with interfaces, tools, and dashboards, but their real expectations rest on the quiet reliability underneath. When someone uploads data to a cloud service, they aren't thinking about network paths, physical hardware, or failover logic. They assume the data will be there when they need it. Meeting that assumption meant investing heavily in the foundational pieces most customers would never see.

Replication was a core example. At the time, enterprise systems were still fragile in many ways. A single point of failure such as a power outage, a network disruption, or a hardware fault could compromise access or data integrity. To avoid that risk, we designed systems to maintain multiple copies of customer data across geographically dispersed zones. If one copy went offline, others could immediately take over. The switch would happen quietly in the background, without a blip in the customer experience. It wasn't flashy, but it was critical.

That kind of decision reflects a broader truth: Many of the most impactful technologies live in the background. They don't draw attention to themselves, but they carry the weight of the business. When they're designed well, no one notices. When they aren't, everything else starts to wobble.

Many of the most impactful technologies live in the background.

But even strong technical decisions can create challenges if they aren't aligned with the broader ecosystem of the organization. One early lesson came from our choice to use Erlang to build my first AWS product's replication system. Technically, it made sense. Erlang was a mature, reliable language, especially strong in distributed systems delivering high performance. From a software engineering perspective, it ticked many boxes.

The business implications were a different story. Erlang was niche. It had a steep learning curve, and few engineers in our hiring pipeline were fluent in it. The style of programming it required was fundamentally different from more widely adopted languages. While the system performed well in isolation, it became difficult to scale and maintain across the team. Hiring became a bottleneck. Training took longer. Updates and maintenance started to slow us down. In hindsight, it was an operational decision that didn't fully account for sustainability.

That experience led to a deeper shift in how we evaluated technology choices. It wasn't enough to ask whether something worked. We had to consider whether it could evolve with us. Could we staff it? Maintain it? Teach it to new engineers? Could it keep up with the business as demands changed? Those questions became part of a decision-making framework we used to pressure-test new ideas before committing to them, the Technology Stack Scorecard. You can access that framework through the QR code included here.

It's tempting to chase innovation purely for its novelty or elegance. But longevity in technology often depends on how well it fits into the ecosystem around it. Speed doesn't come from cutting corners; it comes from making sound decisions early enough that you don't have to rebuild under pressure later. There's wisdom in slowing down just long enough to examine the full picture—technical viability, team capacity, hiring readiness, and long-term adaptability—before moving forward. Think: Slow down to speed up.

Technology doesn't scale on its own. People scale it. And the best infrastructure decisions are the ones that quietly support growth, without forcing constant rework behind the scenes.

The Boeing 747 That Can't Land

At a certain point, every company undergoing transformation starts to feel like it's flying a Boeing 747 that can't land. You're midair, traveling fast, and the engines need an upgrade. The cockpit needs new instrumentation. The fuel system needs to be optimized. And none of it can wait until you're safely on the ground, but in this analogy, the ground doesn't exist. You have customers to serve, deadlines to hit, and systems that can't pause for maintenance. That's the reality of modern enterprise transformation. The work is never done, and the plane never stops flying.

The challenge is that most of the real decisions, the ones that shape whether you're building speed or stalling out, don't look dramatic in the moment. They're often buried inside architecture reviews, team planning meetings, and backlog prioritization sessions. But they matter. Because every time you integrate a new platform, rewrite a workflow, or restructure a process, you're making trade-offs that ripple downstream. And when those trade-offs aren't made deliberately, they accumulate. That's where something called *technical debt* begins in culture, clarity, and continuity. Technical debt describes the hidden cost of making quick, convenient decisions in the short term. Think of it like this: When you're rushing to get a project out the door, you might take a few shortcuts—maybe you don't document the code as well as you should or you build a new feature on an outdated system.

That gets the job done, but it creates a debt that you have to pay back later.

Over time, this debt accumulates. It becomes harder and more expensive to fix bugs, add new features, or integrate with new tools. This can slow down your entire organization, making you less nimble than your competitors and creating a significant competitive disadvantage. In essence, technical debt is the friction that keeps you from moving fast in the future.

This is why I started encouraging teams to use a decision matrix. If you scan the following QR code, you can access the Strategic Investment Framework resource in the Insights Hub. It includes case studies and a detailed explanation on using a decision matrix, but this isn't a complicated tool. It's a structured way to step back and evaluate a technology or system, not just for its immediate performance but for its long-term fit. With a decision matrix, you ask questions such as, What kind of business impact can this generate if we're right? What will it cost us to unwind if we're wrong? Can our current team support and scale it? Can future teams pick it up quickly? Does it reinforce where we're headed, or will it need to be replaced in a year?

The matrix became a forcing mechanism to make the implicit explicit. Instead of relying on gut feel or chasing vendor hype, we mapped choices to a set of criteria that reflected our real-world constraints and goals. That didn't guarantee we'd always get it right (no framework ever does), but it kept us from sleepwalking into decisions we'd later regret. It created a shared language for what made a technology choice good in the context of our mission, not just our metrics.

In organizations where transformation is ongoing, this kind of discipline becomes essential. You can't afford to optimize only for today's needs, because tomorrow is already on its way. And the cost of retooling later, once dependencies stack up, is exponentially higher than getting the foundation right early.

You can't afford to optimize only for today's needs, because tomorrow is already on its way.

The Ship of Theseus analogy captures this well. If you replace every plank on a ship, is it still the same ship? The answer is yes, but only if you're intentional about it. If each replacement is made with awareness of the larger structure, including what it supports, how it connects, and why it matters, then yes, the identity holds. But if you change parts haphazardly, without anchoring them to a clear sense of purpose, you risk ending up with a vessel that no longer knows where it's going, or why.

Technology, teams, and business models evolve. That's not the problem. The problem is when decisions made in isolation start to drag down momentum because they were never designed to hold together in the first place. When that happens, transformation stalls—not because of a lack of effort, but because of a lack of architectural integrity.

In the early days of building AWS, we were intentional about this from the start. We knew that as our teams grew and new features were built, it would be easy to take shortcuts. A team might need a database for a new feature and spin up a small server in a corner. Another team would need a place to store images, so they'd use a different, isolated tool.

We were intentional about avoiding that fragmentation. We understood that technology, teams, and business models would evolve, but that the real problem would be when decisions made in isolation began to drag down our momentum. So, we focused on building a unified architecture from day one. It made things easier, but more importantly, it ensured architectural integrity so that our transformation wouldn't stall tomorrow.

It was the difference between building a single brick that's strong on its own and building a foundation that could hold up an entire skyscraper. We learned that a little intentionality and foresight today is the fastest path to building something great tomorrow.

The Boeing 747 metaphor might sound dramatic, but it's not far off. The businesses that succeed in this kind of transformation aren't just the ones that build fast; they're the ones that build with foresight. That starts with asking better questions and having the courage to slow down, assess the trade-offs, and choose the tools and systems that can evolve with you, not just for you.

Separating the Tectonic from the Trendy

In every wave of technological progress, there's a gravitational pull to chase the shiny new thing. For leaders under pressure to stay ahead, it's tempting to assume that every emerging tool or platform must hold the key to competitive advantage. But the truth is, not all innovation is equal. Some technologies shake the foundation. Others skim the surface. And learning to tell the difference is a core responsibility of modern leadership.

This is where I often draw a distinction between tectonic shifts and ripples. A tectonic shift changes the way you create, deliver, or capture value. It redefines what's possible in your business model, how your teams work, or how your customers engage. A ripple, on the other hand, might create momentary excitement, but it doesn't fundamentally move the business. It's surface-level. Flashy, sometimes loud, but ultimately limited in impact.

Take AI. The right implementations are already reshaping how decisions get made, how customers are served, and how work is done across nearly every function. It's not just optimizing what exists, it's opening doors to what didn't seem possible before. This is the hallmark of a tectonic shift: It enables new capabilities, new value chains, and new ways of competing.

Now compare that to the metaverse. When the metaverse was at its peak buzz, everyone was talking about virtual stores and avatar-based meetings. We saw plenty of businesses rush to explore these concepts. But for most, it was a ripple, not a wave. It was a fascinating distraction.

The core issue wasn't the technology itself. The graphics were incredible and the possibilities seemed endless. The problem was that the technology didn't create immediate, tangible MEx value. Asking someone to put on a headset for a simple team meeting was more friction than it was worth. It didn't make their work better, faster, or more rewarding. It was a novelty that required a huge effort for an incremental gain.

This highlights a key difference between hype and transformation. For the metaverse to become a part of MEx, the technology needs to disappear. It needs to be simple, easy, and frictionless. When that happens, and when a clear, compelling use case emerges that delivers genuine, felt value to individuals, the metaverse will stop being a distraction and start being a foundation for new breakthroughs. We're not there yet, but we're getting closer.

When companies follow hype instead of grounding technology choices in strategic context, the results are predictable. Resources get misallocated. Expectations outrun execution. Leaders lose credibility. And the teams tasked with delivery are left chasing initiatives that never should have been prioritized in the first place. Hype cycles can spark imagination, but they rarely build enduring value.

The real question isn't whether a technology is new. It's whether it's meaningful. Does it unlock new operating models? Can it reduce critical costs in ways that preserve or enhance quality? Will it improve customer or employee experience in a way that drives loyalty or performance? Can it create entirely new revenue streams or reveal untapped market segments?

The real question isn't whether a technology is new. It's whether it's meaningful.

These are the questions that keep you focused on the tectonic, not the trendy. And increasingly, the answer lies not just in the initial implementation but in how the technology enables continuous improvement and adaptation. The most valuable technologies are those that don't just solve today's problems but create platforms for ongoing innovation and responsiveness to changing market conditions. Remember, the key to winning is in skating where the puck is *going to be*, not where it is currently.

Answering these questions is what affords you the kind of clarity that empowers your teams. When people understand why a technology matters, they're more engaged in figuring out how to apply it. They ask better questions and spot smarter use cases. And they stop viewing transformation as a burden and start seeing it as a path to better outcomes. That's the kind of cultural shift that sustains momentum long after the headlines move on.

Technology, in and of itself, is never the answer. It's the enabler. The real value comes from how it changes behavior, workflow, and business mechanics. Not to mention how customer and employee MEs see value or feel positive impact. If it doesn't shift something fundamental, it may not be worth the effort.

Leading Through the Noise

I've seen this play out time and time again: A new technology shows promise, early excitement builds, teams draft proof-of-concept plans. And then everything stalls. Sometimes it's because of overanalysis. Other times it's the weight of competing agendas or pressure from the board to deliver immediate results before the groundwork is even laid. But more often than not, the stall comes from a lack of clarity. Leaders aren't asking the right questions early enough.

If you want to lead through the noise, it starts by framing the right conversation. Not around features, demos, or vendor comparisons but around business impact, long-term viability, and strategic fit. These are the questions I come back to again and again:

WHAT NEW STRATEGIC PLAYS DOES THIS ENABLE?

Technology should unlock something you couldn't do before, such as create new revenue models, improved margin structures, or unique advantages in the way you compete. If the only benefit is incremental efficiency, it may not be worth the lift.

HOW DOES IT RESHAPE THE EMPLOYEE OR CUSTOMER EXPERIENCE?

This is where the real transformation happens. Does it make it easier for people to do great work? Does it improve reliability, personalization, or responsiveness for your customers? If the experience stays the same, you may be automating yesterday's model instead of rethinking it.

ARE WE DATA-READY TO SUPPORT IT AT SCALE?

Even the best algorithms can't function without clean, governed, well-structured data. You need to know whether your systems can provide the inputs needed to get meaningful outputs, and whether you have the talent and infrastructure to manage that responsibly.

ARE THERE COMPLIANCE, ETHICAL, OR SECURITY GAPS?

This can't be an afterthought. In regulated industries, skipping this step can cost millions. But even in more flexible environments, leaders must anticipate where ethical risk might surface. Is the tech explainable? Is it fair? Who's accountable when something goes wrong?

CAN WE SCALE IT BEYOND PROOF OF CONCEPT?

It's easy to get a team to build something cool in a sandbox. What's hard is moving that solution into a real workflow, with real users, where it integrates with legacy systems, supports operational constraints, and produces measurable outcomes. If that scale path isn't clear, the value won't materialize.

In the early days of building AWS, we learned this lesson when we were asked to solve a problem for Amazon's retail business. A team wanted to build a new feature that would allow customers to track their packages in real time. On the surface, it sounded like a simple, cool idea.

A small team built a proof of concept. It worked flawlessly in their sandbox, showing a little truck icon moving across a map. It was beautiful. But when we asked the hard questions, the scale path wasn't clear.

Can it scale beyond a proof of concept? The system was so resource-intensive that if we had rolled it out to millions of customers, it would have been prohibitively expensive and a massive operational risk.

Can it integrate? It didn't connect with the dozen different shipping and logistics partners we used, so the data was often outdated or inaccurate.

Does it produce a measurable outcome? The team couldn't show that this feature would actually increase customer satisfaction or reduce support calls.

We were staring at a classic case of shiny object syndrome. It was a great idea, but it was a great idea built on a fragile foundation. We had to make the difficult decision to kill the project, even though it looked amazing in the demo.

That's when we understood the difference between building a cool gadget and building a platform. We had to be honest with ourselves and kill projects that were technically brilliant but strategically flawed. We realized that asking the hard questions up front is a leader's most important job, even when the answer is difficult to hear.

When leaders fail to ask these questions, the result is often a slide into one of three traps. The first is analysis paralysis, where every decision becomes so weighed down by uncertainty that nothing moves forward. The second is shiny object syndrome, where an organization chases every headline without ever anchoring to real business priorities. And the third is the rush for return, when boards or investors demand short-term ROI from long-term investments, creating a cycle of half-built solutions and unmet expectations.

Escaping those traps requires a different kind of leadership. Not just technical fluency but strategic literacy. The ability to understand the ripple effects of tech choices across functions, timelines, and teams. It takes the courage to change course when new information challenges your assumptions. And just as importantly, it takes the humility to confront when something isn't working, even if it was your idea.

None of this is easy. But this is the work necessary. This is what modern leadership demands. And as technologies evolve at an exponential rate, these questions become essential because they cut through the noise. And they ensure your investments are tied to outcomes that matter.

Reengineering Operations with Intelligence

When most people hear the word *AI*, their minds go to data models, chat interfaces, or smart assistants that answer questions. But AI isn't confined to screens and dashboards. Increasingly, it's finding a body—navigating factory floors, hauling inventory across warehouses, or even maneuvering sidewalks with hot meals tucked inside. Robotics and physical AI represent a critical extension of digital transformation into the physical world, where intelligence meets motion and algorithms begin to carry real weight.

Consider an autonomous mobile robot navigating a manufacturing plant. It doesn't need breaks. It doesn't lose focus mid-shift. It's constantly scanning its environment using computer vision, identifying obstacles, rerouting as needed, and monitoring for anomalies as it moves. And it does this around the clock, with consistency that no human team could match. These robots can transport materials, fetch components, deliver parts between stations, or clean and restock as they go. In the right context, they become part of the operational backbone.

The value of physical AI becomes especially clear in environments that are high-precision or high-risk. Fatigue is a reality in any job that requires repetitive physical motion. Even the most dedicated workers get tired, and in many industrial contexts, fatigue means mistakes. But a robotic system, properly tuned and integrated, doesn't lose steam. It maintains a steady hand, whether it's assembling intricate parts or handling dangerous materials. This has massive implications for safety, quality control, and throughput.

But the implications go well beyond automating labor. These systems introduce a layer of embedded intelligence into physical environments. With advanced sensors and computer vision, robots can detect when something on the line doesn't look right—a component out of alignment, a small crack in a housing, or a temperature change that signals wear. They don't just do; they perceive, analyze, and report. This kind of embedded awareness enables real-time response to potential issues, before they cascade into downtime or defective outputs.

And when you pair robotics with predictive analytics, a new level of operational foresight comes into play. For example, a robot moving materials can feed data into a system that's also modeling inventory needs against incoming demand signals. If a surge of orders comes in and one critical component is in short supply, the system can flag the issue, reprioritize fulfillment, and reroute logistics, all before a human even notices the discrepancy.

For sectors such as logistics, construction, and energy, where both environmental complexity and human risk are high, the upside is even more significant. Robots can enter hazardous areas, handling extreme temperatures, toxic substances, or structurally unsound conditions, without putting human lives at risk. Whether as a drone inspecting a bridge or a crawler navigating the interior of a tank, physical AI adds a layer of resilience and reach that was previously out of the question.

From a business perspective, the impact cuts across cost, speed, and continuity. Labor shortages or high turnover in physical roles no longer brings operations to a halt. Throughput increases without sacrificing quality. Safety improves without slowing down the line. And because these systems are deeply instrumented, they generate vast streams of data that can inform everything from maintenance schedules to future plant design.

But the real unlock comes when leaders view robotics not just as task-doers but as part of a broader system for intelligent infrastructure. That means thinking beyond individual use cases and instead asking: How do these capabilities help us rethink our workflows altogether? What happens when logistics, manufacturing, and maintenance are all connected, physically *and* digitally, by intelligent systems that talk to each other and learn over time?

But the real unlock comes when leaders view robotics not just as task-doers but as part of a broader system for intelligent infrastructure.

That's the transformation underway. Physical AI is redefining the frontline. And for organizations willing to explore these tools with intention, the upside is a fundamentally safer, smarter, and more scalable way to operate in the real world.

Making AI Decisions Transparent and Defensible

If there's one word that separates useful AI from impactful AI at scale, it's *trust*. This means not just technical confidence or low error rates but trust in the full sense of the word: trust from regulators, your board, your customers, and the people who use the systems every day.

Trust, after all, is built on understanding. And in the era of intelligent automation, that's where explainability comes in.

Explainable AI means pulling back the curtain and making sure that for every recommendation, prediction, or automated decision, a human can understand how it was made. That includes knowing what data went in, how the system processed that data, and what logic led to the result. It doesn't mean simplifying every model down to a few if-then statements but rather being able to trace the steps and audit the outcome in a way that makes sense to someone who didn't build the system.

This matters because AI is increasingly making decisions that affect people's lives and livelihoods. Consider a lending decision. If an AI model declines a loan application, can you explain why? Was it a credit score issue? A mismatch in address data? A pattern in payment history that triggered a risk flag? And more importantly, can the applicant understand that explanation, and challenge it if something's off?

Or take identity verification. Two utility bills with slightly different address formats shouldn't disqualify someone from proving who they are. But if a model isn't built or monitored carefully, that kind of inconsistency might look like fraud. It's not enough to say, "the system said no." Organizations need to be able to say why, show how the conclusion was reached, and correct the system when it gets it wrong.

That's where trustworthiness comes in. Explainability is part of the puzzle. But to be truly trustworthy, AI systems need mechanisms for validation, human oversight, and fairness. That requires building workflows in which decisions can be reviewed and reversed, and tracking outcomes to identify unintended bias. And it means bringing humans into the loop as active stewards of how AI is used.

In high-stakes contexts, this becomes nonnegotiable. A glitch in a marketing algorithm might waste ad spend. A glitch in a health-care triage tool could delay critical care. Trustworthiness suddenly becomes a requirement for responsible deployment. And it's increasingly becoming a legal requirement as well. Emerging regulations around AI fairness, data protection, and algorithmic accountability are clear: If you can't explain it, you probably shouldn't be using it.

Emerging regulations around AI fairness, data protection, and algorithmic accountability are clear: If you can't explain it, you probably shouldn't be using it.

But beyond compliance, explainability is essential for internal adoption. If teams don't understand how an AI model works, they're unlikely to use it—or worse, they'll rely on it blindly. Both are dangerous. The goal is intelligent augmentation, where humans and machines work together, each strengthening the other's capabilities. That only happens when trust is built into the system, not layered on afterward.

This is also a leadership challenge. As AI becomes more embedded in business processes, leaders will increasingly be asked to vouch for decisions made by machines. They must know when to trust the model and when to dig deeper. Whatever the case, humans must always be in the loop.

Explainability enables speeding up the adoption of AI. When people understand how decisions are made, they're more likely to embrace change. That's how you unlock scale.

In the AI era, every decision made by a machine still has a human fingerprint on it. The question is whether that fingerprint reflects care, clarity, and accountability. If it does, congratulations; you're building the kind of trust that turns technology into transformation.

Beyond the Curve: Redefining Competitive Advantage

While many organizations are still catching up to today's AI capabilities, the most transformative breakthroughs are already taking shape beyond the edges of mainstream adoption. These are foundational shifts, ones that promise to redefine how work is done, how value is created, and how companies compete in the decades ahead.

To lead effectively in this new era, leaders must understand not only what these technologies do but how they change the rules of the game.

ARTIFICIAL GENERAL INTELLIGENCE: THE NEXT QUANTUM LEAP IN INTELLIGENCE

Artificial general intelligence (AGI) represents an evolution in intelligent systems. Unlike specialized AI capabilities that excel in specific domains, AGI can understand, learn, and apply intelligence across *any* intellectual task, much like a human mind with the expertise of a professional with a master's degree in the subject matter. It takes AI from being a faster calculator to being a general-purpose genius that can adapt, reason, innovate, and problem-solve across disciplines, constantly learning from new data and experiences. This is where machines become truly autonomous thinkers.

Why It Matters for Business Transformation

AGI represents the ultimate frontier of business transformation. It unlocks an unprecedented digital velocity in problem-solving and innovation, tackling complex, multidomain challenges currently intractable for human teams or narrow AI. This isn't just about efficiency; it's about having a tireless, adaptable, and infinitely scalable intelligent partner that can contribute to *any* strategic endeavor, from inventing new products to designing entire business models. It's the ultimate engine for creating insurmountable digital moats through accelerated insight and autonomous action, fundamentally redefining how value is created and captured in the data-driven economy.

Potential Real-World Applications and Mapping

The applications of AGI extend far beyond current imaginations, but we can foresee profound shifts across every sector:

- **Universal personal and executive assistants:** Imagine an intelligent technology partner that understands your preferences, context, and goals across *all* domains. AGI could function as an always-on personal or executive assistant, handling any complex task. This fundamentally redefines individual productivity and frees up human capital for higher-level creative and strategic endeavors.

- **Innovation and R&D:** AGI could act as a universal scientist or engineer, rapidly generating and testing hypotheses across disciplines (e.g., designing breakthrough sustainable materials or inventing new forms of energy with exponential speed by analyzing global research data and simulating outcomes).

- **Automated strategic planning and decision-making:** AGI could analyze global markets, geopolitical data, and competitive intelligence in real time to autonomously propose, refine, and execute complex business strategies, identifying threats and opportunities far beyond human capacity.

- **Hyperpersonalized universal services:** AGI could deliver truly adaptive, always-on, holistic personalized experiences for customers and employees across every interaction, learning from every piece of data to optimize engagement, well-being, and individual productivity in a way currently impossible.

Potential Misunderstandings and Misapplications

As profound as AGI's promise is, the conversation is riddled with critical misunderstandings. The most common mistake in the conversation about AGI is the Skynet fallacy. This is the overestimation and misdirection that comes from focusing on Hollywood-style rogue AI taking over the world. While existential risks require serious, long-term philosophical attention, this often distracts from the immediate, tangible challenge of ensuring responsible AI governance for *narrow* AI today. AGI won't be a simple villain; it will be a potent tool that demands rigorous human-defined purpose and ethics, designed for alignment.

Dismissing AGI as too far off to care about now is another fatal strategic error. The foundational steps for AGI (e.g., advanced data infrastructure, ethical AI frameworks, autonomous agents) are being built *today*. Waiting ensures you'll be buried in the digital quicksand when it becomes mainstream, having missed the opportunity to shape its development and harness its power.

How then, you might ask, do we audit, regulate, or even understand an intelligent system that can learn and reason across *all* domains? The challenge of explainable AI becomes exponentially more complex, demanding robust governance and human oversight protocols. Ensuring data transparency and interpretability for a truly general intelligence remains ambiguous, but it should be at the forefront of every leader's mind.

In this way, ensuring AGI's goals remain aligned with human values and business objectives will be paramount. Without careful ethical design, continuous monitoring, and robust off switches, an AGI optimizing for efficiency might achieve it in ways unintended or undesirable by its human creators, potentially leading to catastrophic outcomes. This is the ultimate leadership imperative in the age of intelligent technology.

Beyond AI

For all the attention AI rightly gets, it's only one piece of a much larger transformation puzzle. To lead through this next wave of innovation, organizations need to widen their lens. Because while AI may be the most visible force shaping the future, it's not acting alone. It's converging with a set of foundational technologies that are quietly changing the way we operate, build, and deliver value. These are the infrastructure shifts that create leverage. Ignore them, and your strategy becomes brittle. Understand them, and you start to unlock the full spectrum of digital advantage.

Start with the Internet of Things (IoT). The IoT gives the physical world a digital voice. It allows machines, buildings, vehicles, and everyday objects to collect and share data in real time. For leaders, this unlocks new streams of operational insight. A connected factory floor can identify bottlenecks as they emerge. A smart logistics network can reroute assets to avoid delays. Even commercial real estate can dynamically adjust energy use based on occupancy and weather patterns. The IoT brings situational awareness to operations that were previously silent.

But streaming that much real-time data requires a new approach to processing. That's where edge computing enters the equation.

Rather than sending every bit of data back to a central cloud, edge systems process information closer to where it's collected—in the warehouse, in the store, even inside a delivery vehicle. This enables faster decision-making, reduces latency, and helps maintain continuity in environments where connectivity isn't always reliable. For industries such as manufacturing, healthcare, and retail, edge computing is a performance enabler.

Your IoT data creates more than internal efficiencies; it's the raw material for entirely new revenue streams. Consider how fitness trackers have already evolved from simple step counters to personalized health coaches, offering premium services based on individual data. The trends you uncover, the hyper-personalization you enable, the proactive recommendations you can offer—these are all opportunities for new, high-margin services that your competitors can't easily replicate. Or, in other words, these are opportunities to create a ME(x) for your business model. Because beyond simply connecting devices, IoT connects intelligence to business value. Your IoT data is not a cost, but the fuel for your next profit center.

Then there's the immersive internet. Think beyond entertainment and gaming. These technologies, such as augmented reality, virtual reality, and mixed reality, are redefining how people learn, collaborate, and engage. In enterprise contexts, immersive tools allow teams to simulate complex processes, visualize designs before they're built, and deliver training experiences that are more intuitive and memorable than anything a slide deck can offer. Whether you're onboarding new employees, walking customers through a product demo, or redesigning a physical space, immersive tech helps bridge the gap between concept and comprehension.

THE IMMERSIVE INTERNET: FROM SCREENS TO WORLDS

The internet as we know it is a two-dimensional experience. We look at websites, scroll through feeds, and watch videos. But the next wave of transformation—the real breakthrough—is the immersive internet. Perhaps that sounds like futuristic fantasy, but the tangible use cases are here today, redefining how businesses interact with customers and train employees.

Think of it as the ultimate evolution of MEx. We are moving from a world of information on a screen to a world where we are *in* the information. This isn't just about virtual reality headsets; it's about a new layer of spatial, interactive, and personalized digital life that can be accessed from anywhere. Imagine a company no longer just being a website but a world you can step into. This promises to redefine what it means to engage with customers, collaborate with teams, and build a business. The core principle is removing friction by bridging the digital and physical worlds—creating an experience so intuitive, so effortless, that the technology disappears.

The Real-World Impact on Business

The immersive internet is set to fundamentally change how we work, interact, and create value.

- **Travel and hospitality:** The ultimate evolution of a travel agent is an AI that's also a navigator. Imagine a virtual avatar travel agent helping you plan a trip to

Dubai by understanding your preferences, creating an itinerary, and booking everything for you.

- **Retail and e-commerce:** Imagine a customer not just browsing a product page but walking into a virtual storefront. They can see a product from every angle, customize it in real time, and even "try it on." Brands can create a deeply personalized and memorable shopping experience that is far more compelling than a flat photo.

- **Customer service:** The most frustrating support calls are often about navigating a complex interface. An immersive environment allows an agent to "walk" alongside a customer in a shared space, pointing out what to click and how to solve an issue. This turns a complex, multistep process into a simple shared experience.

The Path Forward: What Leaders Should Do Now

The immersive internet is a foundational shift, not just a trend. Escaping the shiny object trap requires us to be deliberate. The global immersive technology market is projected to reach $638.69 billion by 2028, with a compound annual growth rate of 42.5 percent.[15] This isn't a market you can afford to ignore. This technology is a new layer of spatial, interactive, and personalized digital life. It's a human solution to a human problem, and the question is: **Are you ready to build the new reality for your organization?**

---

15   Research and Markets, "Immersive Technology Research Report 2024: Market to Reach $638.69 Billion in 2028 at a CAGR of 42.5% - Global Long-Term Forecast to 2033," *Yahoo Finance*, September 10, 2024, https://finance.yahoo.com/news/immersive-technology-research-report-2024-151800942.html.

- **Start with the user's journey, not the technology:** Don't build a virtual world just because you can. Ask, What part of our customer journey is the most frustrating, and how could an immersive experience dramatically simplify it? The value must be felt and experienced by the customer, not just by the developers who built it.
- **Focus on friction reduction:** The goal isn't to create a complex new world. The goal is to make the technology disappear. Prioritize experiences that are easy, simple, and require minimal effort to engage with. The technology must serve the user, not the other way around.

Blockchain: The Shared Source of Truth

Trust, meanwhile, is being redefined by blockchain and distributed ledger technologies. Despite the noise around cryptocurrencies, the core value of blockchain is clear: It provides a secure, auditable, and decentralized way to record and verify transactions.

The internet as we know it is a world of copied information, where a single source can be altered or erased. Blockchain is different. Think of it as a digital notary that provides a shared, unchangeable record of truth that everyone can trust. No single person or company owns it, which means it can't be tampered with. It creates a single source of truth that every party can trust implicitly.

In my experience building platforms at AWS and Microsoft, the greatest friction in business often comes from a lack of trust between different parties. Blockchain solves that problem, allowing you to build new business models and relationships based on a shared, immutable reality.

The Real-World Impact on Business

Blockchain is set to fundamentally change how we transact, collaborate, and share value.

Imagine a contract that automates your business logic. A smart contract is a self-executing agreement that automatically triggers a payment when the conditions are met. This eliminates manual friction, reduces costs, and speeds up business cycles from weeks to minutes. For any business that moves physical goods, blockchain can be a game-changer. It can create an immutable record of a product's journey from its origin to the end customer.

The MEx promises a world of hyperpersonalization, but that requires trust. Blockchain can give individuals a secure, self-sovereign digital identity, where they control their personal data. Instead of trusting a company with their data, they can grant permission for specific, temporary access, creating a new paradigm of secure, personalized engagement.

What Leaders Should Do Now

The conversation around blockchain has been full of hype and false starts, but the technology is now ready for prime time.

- **Start with the friction of trust:** Don't ask, Where can we use blockchain? Ask, Where is our greatest source of friction, inefficiency, or risk due to a lack of trust between us and our partners, suppliers, or customers? This anchors your strategy to a real business problem, not just a cool technology.

- **Think in terms of a network:** A blockchain is only as powerful as the network that uses it. The value comes from getting all the right players—your suppliers, partners, and customers—on the same shared source of truth. Your strategy should be about building an ecosystem, not just a single-company solution.

Quantum Computing: The Next Leap in Problem-Solving

The computers we use today are built on a simple foundation: bits. A bit is a switch that is either on or off, a 1 or a 0. This is the bedrock of digital logic.

Quantum computing is different. It's built on qubits, which can be both a 1 and a 0 at the same time. Think of a bit as a coin that can only land on heads or tails. A qubit is a coin that is constantly spinning, holding every possible state in between. This fundamental difference means a quantum computer doesn't just calculate one path; it explores countless possibilities simultaneously. This promises to redefine what it means to solve a problem. It's a whole new way of thinking that will unlock solutions to problems that are currently impossible for any computer we have today.

The Real-World Impact on Business

Quantum computing is set to fundamentally change how we innovate, optimize, and secure our businesses. It won't replace our current computers, but it will work alongside them to solve our most complex challenges. This is our new competitive frontier.

Imagine simulating the molecular structure of a new drug to see how it interacts with a disease. A classical computer would take a lifetime to calculate these variables. A quantum computer can do it in minutes, dramatically accelerating the path to new medical breakthroughs. Or consider complex portfolios and risk management. A quantum computer can analyze millions of data points simultaneously, finding the most optimal investment strategies or detecting fraudulent activity with a new level of precision and speed.

From designing more efficient batteries for electric vehicles to creating new catalysts for clean energy, quantum computers can simulate the behavior of new materials at the atomic level, which is a game-changer for manufacturing and engineering.

What Leaders Should Do Now

The conversation around quantum computing is full of hype, but the technology is now ready for serious strategic consideration:

- **Educate the C-suite:** This is a strategic-level conversation, not just a technical one. Your leadership team needs to understand that this technology is a potential key to solving your most valuable, currently unsolvable problems.

- **Start with the "impossible" problem:** Don't ask, Where can we use quantum computing? Ask, What is a problem in our business that we currently cannot solve with any computer, and what would the value be if we could? Again, anchor your strategy in real business outcomes, not just cool technologies.

Whether you're exploring the immersive internet, blockchain, or quantum computing, the strategic imperative remains the same: this is a scale question, not a one-off opportunity. Resist the temptation to build isolated, siloed projects that demonstrate technical capability but lack organizational impact. Instead, design foundational infrastructure that can support future initiatives across each of these transformative technologies. The immersive internet requires spatial computing frameworks that can evolve; blockchain demands interoperable trust architectures; quantum computing needs hybrid classical-quantum systems that can grow with the technology. This intentionality today—building for tomorrow's possibilities rather than today's proof-of-concept—is the fastest path to creating a truly great, resilient, and trustworthy business in an era of convergent technologies.

How to Evaluate Emerging Technologies with Purpose

When leaders face the onslaught of emerging technologies, the natural instinct is often one of two extremes: Either chase every shiny object or retreat behind the comfort of "wait and see." Neither approach works, not when the pace of change accelerates faster than traditional planning cycles. The real work is in finding a disciplined way to evaluate what matters, when it matters, and how it matters to your business. That's the difference between reactive trend-chasing and deliberate, advantage-building strategy.

The question isn't whether these technologies will reshape industries. Many already are. The question is which technologies can reshape your business, and what strategic role they play in that evolution. To answer that, you need a clear lens for evaluation. Here's a place to start:

First, ask: Does this enable entirely new revenue streams? IoT, for example, has allowed industrial manufacturers to shift from product sales to as-a-service models, turning onetime transactions into recurring revenue. When a technology enables you to make money in a fundamentally different way, it deserves a closer look.

Second, ask: Does it deliver a breakthrough in efficiency? Some technologies don't change what you offer, but they radically improve how you operate. Think about edge computing reducing latency in autonomous systems or additive manufacturing collapsing prototyping cycles from months to days. If the gain is significant enough to shift your margins or scale, that's strategic.

Third, ask: Does it help mitigate existential risk while improving the experience for each individual ME we serve—whether customer, employee, or partner? Trust, security, and operational resilience are becoming competitive differentiators. Blockchain may not drive revenue directly, but if it helps you ensure traceability in your supply chain or prevent fraudulent transactions, its value is real. And with quantum computing on the horizon, encryption standards themselves could be at risk. Awareness today helps avoid disruption tomorrow.

Fourth, ask: Does it open the door to a fundamentally better customer or employee experience? Immersive technologies, for example, allow people to engage with products, ideas, and environments in more intuitive ways. That value goes well beyond a UX upgrade. It can drive loyalty, increase learning retention, and reduce errors, which are outcomes that compound over time.

Once you've clarified potential value, the next filter is timing. Not every technology needs to be acted on immediately. But it does need to be watched with intent. To assess readiness, evaluate time to value and ask: How long before this capability pays off? Factor in the competitive clock: Will waiting cede advantage to a faster-moving rival? And don't overlook organizational readiness: Do you have the talent, systems, and cultural posture to adopt it well?

This last one is often the hardest. A technology may be strategically relevant and competitively urgent, but if your teams aren't prepared to integrate it, the result will be noise, fatigue, or worse, failure that breeds cynicism.

That's why deliberate experimentation matters. Not every innovation has to scale immediately. But every organization needs a place to test, learn, and refine. Set up a lightweight pilot. Identify measurable outcomes. Create clear feedback loops. And most importantly, tie every experiment back to your core strategy.

Beware the lure of novelty, because new doesn't always mean better. There's a difference between being first and being ready. Being first without readiness is a gamble. Being ready and intentional is a strategy.

A technology may be strategically relevant and competitively urgent, but if your teams aren't prepared to integrate it, the result will be noise, fatigue, or worse, failure that breeds cynicism.

Infrastructure, Modularity, and the Netflix Moment

If strategy is the why and technology is the what, infrastructure is the how. It's the invisible scaffolding beneath your business that determines whether innovation takes root or slides into chaos. And the truth is, most organizations are still trying to plant future-ready ideas in yesterday's soil.

You can't run intelligent operations, let alone deploy emerging technologies, on brittle, monolithic systems built for another era. The businesses that move the fastest today are those that invested early in modularity, data accessibility, and API-first architecture. Not because it was trendy, but because it was necessary for scale, speed, and change.

APIs—application programming interfaces—are essentially the digital connectors that let different software systems talk to each other. They're the architectural outlets of your business.

Just as an electrical outlet provides a standard way to plug in a new device without having to rewire the entire building, APIs provide a standard way to plug in a new capability. This is how you avoid technical debt and enable speed. Instead of your teams having to build a new data connection from scratch every time, they can simply use a well-defined API.

My experience building platforms at AWS and Microsoft taught me APIs are the key to creating an ecosystem. They are the invisible infrastructure that lets you easily connect with new partners, launch new services, and scale without breaking the system. They are the architectural foundation for a fast, nimble business.

The biggest misconception in digital transformation is that it's about buying the latest software. It's not. The real challenge is architectural. Modular infrastructure is the solution.

Think of it like building with LEGO blocks instead of carving a statue out of a single block of marble. It means designing your systems in independent blocks that can be replaced, upgraded, or scaled without affecting the rest of the business.

In my experience, this is the key to agility. When one part of your business needs to evolve, the others don't have to break. Teams can innovate and deploy new services without waiting for a twelve-month system overhaul. Most importantly, this gives you the agility to respond to market shifts with precision instead of panic. It's the architectural foundation that allows you to move fast and be flexible in an ever-changing world.

Modular infrastructure doesn't mean buying the latest software or layering on more tools. It means designing your systems in blocks that can be replaced, upgraded, or scaled independently.

APIs let teams connect services, share data, and build new workflows without having to reinvent the wheel. This is how you avoid the cost of complexity and how you build once and adapt many times. At AWS, we saw APIs as a way to empower our customers. We gave them the permission to build, innovate, and connect their systems in a standardized way. It was the key to building a platform, not just a product.

But modularity without governance becomes entropy. That's why intelligent infrastructure is as much about how you manage as what you deploy. Do you have clear protocols around data access? Are privacy and security built into the foundation, not bolted on as afterthoughts? Can your systems support the oversight and explainability required in an AI-powered world?

But modularity without governance becomes entropy.

The more flexible your infrastructure, the more resilient your operations become. If a new business model emerges, can your systems support it? If a compliance regulation changes, can you adapt without grinding to a halt? If your competitors move first, can you catch up? Or perhaps leapfrog?

This brings us to Netflix. Before it was a global content powerhouse, it was a DVD rental company mailing disks in red envelopes. But instead of riding that model to its peak and plateau, the company made a decision few others were willing to make. It bet on streaming, not as an add-on but as a future. And to support that future, it rebuilt its infrastructure to handle global scale, variable demand, and rapid content delivery.

Netflix didn't wait for broadband to become ubiquitous. It didn't wait for user behavior to fully shift. It started building anyway and separated core services. Then it moved to the cloud, designing systems to evolve so that when the moment came, it would be ready. And Netflix's AWS architecture wasn't just designed to stream video. It was designed to own the entire viewer experience—from predicting what you want to watch (AI recommendations), to delivering it instantly (infrastructure), to handling your payment and support. By controlling the entire journey, Netflix made itself indispensable. That's why its churn rates are manageable, and why it holds an insurmountable competitive moat today. Even when the competition finally arrived, Netflix dominated.

That story we all know is a masterclass in strategic foresight. It's a reminder that the boldest moves don't always start with technology but with belief that the way things are isn't the way they have to be. Belief that future advantage is earned in the quiet, architectural decisions most customers never see.

So if you're serious about transformation, don't just look at what you're building. Look at what you're building *on*. Start by identifying a core human activity or workflow in your industry—it could be engineering design, supply chain logistics, or even professional education—and ask a challenging question: How can we use intelligent technology to own the entire customer journey, from start to finish?

By moving from providing a single piece of the puzzle to owning the entire outcome, you transition your company from being an optional expense to being the essential utility that enables your customer's success.

That is the ultimate goal of business transformation.

FIVE STEPS TO TAKE NOW

The pace of change can make any leader feel like they're behind. But technology transformation means laying the right foundation, asking sharper questions, and making choices today that compound value tomorrow. These five steps will help you move from insight to action, one deliberate decision at a time.

Step 1: Map Your Infrastructure's Flexibility

Pick one critical business workflow, something that touches customers, employees, or partners every day. Ask your tech team to diagram the systems that support it and highlight:

- Which components are modular and swappable
- Which ones require full-system changes to update
- Where APIs enable (or block) data flow

You don't need to be a technologist to ask these questions. But you do need to understand where rigidity is limiting agility. Once you know, you can begin planning the shift toward infrastructure that adapts.

Step 2: Run a Tech Foresight Session

Convene a sixty-minute strategy sprint with a cross-functional group—leaders from operations, IT, marketing, finance, and the front lines. Frame the conversation around three questions:

- What technologies are we already using that we're not getting full value from?
- What emerging tech have we dismissed too quickly or not explored at all?
- What internal decisions would we need to make now to prepare for change later?

By doing this, you're building strategic muscle memory, developing a team that can scan, sense, and respond to what's coming.

Step 3: Define Your "No-Fly Zone"

Not every trend deserves your attention. In fact, a clear sense of what *not* to pursue is as valuable as a prioritized tech list. Create a short policy with your leadership team that outlines:

- Technologies you'll avoid (for now) because of low business fit
- Criteria for experimentation (e.g., time to value, use case clarity, ethical implications)
- Guardrails to prevent shiny-object spending

This gives teams the confidence to explore without drifting into distraction.

Step 4: Evaluate One System for Explainability

Choose one AI- or data-powered system your organization relies on. This could be anything from an internal chatbot to a customer segmentation tool. Ask:

- What inputs drive its decisions?
- Can a nontechnical team member explain how it works?
- Who's accountable for the decisions it influences?

If the answers aren't clear, it's time to build in transparency. The long-term trust of your employees and customers depends on it.

Step 5: Spot the Next Netflix Moment

In your next board or executive meeting, carve out fifteen minutes to reflect on this question: Where are we still mailing DVDs when the future is already streaming?

This is your prompt to examine areas of the business that feel familiar, functional, and vulnerable. Don't wait for disruption to force your hand. Identify one product, process, or revenue model that's overdue for reinvention. Then assign a small team to explore what reinvention could look like, without the pressure of immediate ROI. Remember: You can't predict every wave. That's why you build a business that can ride any wave that comes your way.

CHAPTER SEVEN

DATA-DRIVEN DECISION-MAKING

The goal is to turn data into information and information into insight.

—CARLY FIORINA

> **Your Mission Possible Blueprint:** You can't automate what you don't understand. And you can't scale what you can't trust. This chapter is your blueprint for building the data foundation required to unlock real business transformation—from operational efficiency to personalized experiences to intelligent AI. You'll walk away with a strategic playbook for turning fragmented, inconsistent, or incomplete data into a source of speed, precision, and enterprise-wide confidence.

YOU CAN'T BUILD a skyscraper on a swamp. I've seen too many leaders pour millions into sophisticated software, automation platforms, and AI systems, only to watch those investments falter because the data foundation underneath them was weak or chaotic. Everyone wants the skyline view—the sweeping transformation, the intelligent forecasting, the operational precision. But most of the time, the real work starts far below ground level, where the hard, unglamorous task of data remediation happens.

One project that continues to stay with me began with frustration and ended in transformation. A global manufacturer had just implemented an advanced planning system intended to optimize everything from forecasting to supplier coordination. But almost immediately, the system produced confusing results—delayed orders, off-base forecasts, and erratic inventory data. The issue wasn't the tool itself but the quality of the data feeding it. Inventory records were mismatched, lead times were based on guesswork, and sales data was riddled with errors. It became clear that the real challenge wasn't technological. It was *foundational.*

We paused the rollout and turned our attention to the root problem. Warehouse teams verified inventory shelf by shelf. Lead times were recalibrated, sales anomalies corrected, and promotional data standardized across departments. We established a master data structure to serve as the single source of truth. It was an intensive process, but once the data was clean, the entire system began to perform. Forecasts aligned with reality. Inventory became leaner and smarter. Customer satisfaction rose. That experience confirmed a simple truth: No system, no matter how sophisticated, can outperform the quality of the data it runs on. Transformation starts not with tools but with trust in your data, your process, and your foundation.

When we scaled AWS, for instance, data readiness was never treated as a background task. It was a strategic imperative. Every new service we launched—whether it was around compute power, storage, billing, or customer usage—was designed on top of a meticulously maintained data backbone. That's what made automation possible. That's what enabled us to predict customer needs, bill accurately for services used, and scale resources in real time. And that's why the platform could support the explosive growth we saw year after year.

Many organizations don't realize this until they're well into their transformation journey. They invest in sophisticated tools and talented teams. They plan for machine learning, computer vision, and intelligent automation, whether implementing these capabilities for the first time or enhancing existing systems. But they don't stop to ask whether their data is actually ready to support any of that. The hard truth is, most of the friction you're feeling—delayed timelines, inconsistent reporting, or stakeholder confusion—isn't because your tech stack is underpowered. It's because your data is unprepared.

And this isn't just a technical issue. It's a leadership issue. If the foundation isn't sound, it falls to leadership to acknowledge it and create the conditions to fix it. This means dedicating time, resources, and top-level support to the messy work of data cleaning, integration, and governance. It means resisting the urge to leap into high-visibility innovation projects before the groundwork is done. No matter how good your AI models are, or how slick your interface looks, unreliable data will lead to unreliable outcomes. And when that happens, trust erodes, confidence fades, and progress stalls.

If the business is the skyscraper, the data is the soil, the bedrock, the rebar, and the concrete. Without it, nothing stands for long.

Clean Data, Clear Decisions

In the rush to modernize, most organizations overlook the simplest reason why transformation efforts stall: People don't trust the numbers. They're looking at reports and dashboards, but what they're really doing is asking, Can I rely on this? If they're not sure, they fall back on workarounds—manual reconciliation, personal spreadsheets, hallway whispers. And once that happens, you're no longer running the business on data. You're running it on doubt.

I've seen this up close, not just in startups, but in some of the world's largest, most complex enterprises. One retailer I worked with had troves of data coming in from all directions—stores, websites, call centers, mobile apps. In theory, the business had everything it needed to deliver a seamless, personalized experience to each customer. But in reality, none of the systems talked to each other. Store teams had one version of the ME customer, the digital team had another, and customer service had a third. Everyone was making decisions, but no one was working from the same truth.

That kind of fragmentation creates more than just operational inefficiency. It creates organizational friction. Marketing runs a campaign based on online behavior, unaware that the customer already returned the item in-store. Operations overstock one location, not realizing MEx demand patterns have shifted. Leaders argue not about what to do but about which data to believe. Momentum dies in meetings like those. I've been in rooms where millions of dollars of opportunity were put on hold simply because no one could agree whether the underlying data was accurate.

Now contrast that with what we learned scaling AWS. Cloud infrastructure, by its very nature, doesn't allow room for ambiguity. Every service, every feature, every customer-facing change had to be built on a foundation of precise, real-time data. We were operating at a level where even a single misreported usage metric could cascade into overprovisioned resources, billing errors, or performance degradation. When you're serving hundreds of thousands of customers, each with different usage patterns, geographies, compliance requirements, and support needs, there's no margin for approximation.

To make effective scaling possible, data governance was a core business priority. Ownership was clearly defined. Quality standards were explicit. Audit mechanisms were built into the system. And every team—from infrastructure to billing to customer success—knew where the authoritative data lived and how to access it. That clarity is what made scale possible. It's what allowed automation to work, integrations to succeed, and new innovations to launch without creating chaos downstream.

The same principle applies across any organization trying to operate at speed. If you want to move fast without breaking things, your data needs to be trustworthy, accessible, and structured from the start. That only happens when leaders make it a priority.

Reliable data reduces friction across the enterprise. When teams trust the numbers, they stop second-guessing each other. They spend less time reconciling and more time executing. Meetings shift from debates over accuracy to alignment around action. And when that happens, you create real business velocity, the kind that compounds.

But none of this is possible without governance—lean, purposeful, clearly defined processes that ensure your most critical data is always accurate, consistent, and well understood. This means deciding who owns which data domains and implementing validation rules at the point of entry. And most importantly, it means building a culture in which data stewardship is taken seriously at every level of the business.

The organizations that struggle are the ones that treat data quality as a onetime project when something breaks rather than something to protect as you scale. But the truth is, bad data hurts much more than your systems. It hurts your credibility. When your executive team loses faith in the reports, when frontline teams stop relying on the tools, when customers receive experiences that feel inconsistent or impersonal, those aren't IT problems. Those are business risks.

When your executive team loses faith in the reports, when frontline teams stop relying on the tools, when customers receive experiences that feel inconsistent or impersonal, those aren't IT problems. Those are business risks.

If your vision is to deliver hyperpersonalized experiences, run autonomous agents, or build immersive environments, then the data driving those capabilities needs to be pristine. Dirty data pollutes every layer of your transformation effort. And it's especially dangerous because the problem is often *invisible* until it causes real damage.

So the question leaders should be asking isn't whether they have enough data. It's whether they have the right structures in place to govern it. Can you trace the origin of a key business metric? Do all systems reference the same definitions? Are updates validated, or do they drift over time? Are people confident enough in the numbers to act without hesitation? To help answer these questions, I've developed

the Data Readiness Assessment, available on the Insights Hub, which you can access through this QR code.

Data governance, when done well, becomes the invisible architecture that allows your organization to move with speed and precision. It's the connective tissue between vision and execution. And it's the reason some companies continue to scale while others stall out under the weight of their own complexity.

The Power of a Unified View

Many transformation efforts stall not because of the technology itself, but because people don't trust the data behind it. When teams question the accuracy of reports or dashboards, they default to manual workarounds—personal spreadsheets, offline conversations, and gut instincts. This erosion of trust creates organizational friction, where energy is spent reconciling different versions of the truth instead of aligning around clear action.

I've seen this across companies of every size. One large retailer had all the data it needed—across stores, apps, and support centers—but lacked integration. Each team worked from a different version of the customer, creating misaligned decisions and missed opportunities. Contrast that with the rigor we practiced scaling AWS, where every system was built on a foundation of precise, governed, real-time data. Ownership was clear, definitions were consistent, and trust in the numbers made speed and scale possible.

That's the lesson: Real velocity doesn't come from more data but from data that is reliable, structured, and stewarded. Good governance is what turns vision into execution. When data is trusted, teams move faster, collaborate more easily, and deliver better outcomes. But when it's fragmented or questionable, momentum stalls and credibility erodes. The organizations that scale are the ones that treat data as infrastructure—something to invest in, protect, and build upon every day.

Building Accountability into the System

Too often, organizations treat data initiatives like IT projects. They assign a tool, a timeline, and a team, then assume the problem has been solved. But transforming how a business uses data is an organizational endeavor, not just a technical one. Tools may enable change, but systems of accountability sustain it. Without clear roles, responsibilities, and decision rights, even the best data platforms will eventually fail under the weight of ambiguity and dysfunction.

Without clear roles, responsibilities, and decision rights, even the best data platforms will eventually fail under the weight of ambiguity and dysfunction.

This is why building data accountability is a nonnegotiable. It begins by establishing shared ownership for data across the enterprise, and aligning that ownership with the operational structures that drive decision-making. In practical terms, this means asking and answering a series of uncomfortable but necessary questions. Who owns this data? Who is responsible for its accuracy, quality, and security? Who ensures that it evolves as the business evolves?

One way to bring clarity is by creating a data council—a cross-functional group of leaders from key departments who come together to shape and steward the organization's overall data strategy. The purpose of this council isn't to centralize power or become another bureaucratic layer. It's to bring competing interests into a shared conversation and to align data initiatives to enterprise-wide goals. When you involve leaders from marketing, sales, finance, supply chain, and customer service in the same forum, you prevent the common trap of optimizing data for one function at the expense of another. You also create a foundation for consistent definitions and performance measures, which is critical in environments where metrics drive accountability.

But councils alone aren't enough. Someone must be clearly accountable for the integrity of the data itself. That's where data owners come in. These are leaders responsible for specific data domains—customer, product, financials, operations—and they have the mandate to define how data should be collected, structured, validated, and accessed. This isn't about holding someone liable when things go wrong. It's about empowering leaders to proactively govern the information their teams rely on, and to advocate for improvements when gaps are discovered. If, for instance, customer address data is inconsistent across systems, the designated data owner for customer information should have both the visibility and the authority to fix it.

Equally important is managing the lifecycle of change. Every time a system gets upgraded, every time a new report is requested, and every time a team introduces a new way of capturing or displaying information, there is a ripple effect across the data ecosystem. Many organizations underestimate the degree to which even a seemingly minor update can break downstream processes. To counter this, leaders need to adopt the mindset of proactive change management. That means communicating not just what is changing but why it matters, who it affects, and what outcomes it will support.

The more you operationalize change with this level of transparency, the more likely you are to bring people along for the journey. People don't resist change because they're lazy or outdated. They resist it when they feel excluded from the process or when they can't connect the dots between a new way of working and the value it creates. That's why it's critical to frame change in terms of what matters most: how it helps teams deliver for customers, reduce friction, and make better decisions with less effort.

And finally, no system of accountability is complete without investing in ongoing support. New dashboards and tools may look sleek on the surface, but if the teams using them don't understand how the numbers are generated, or don't trust the source, adoption stalls. Support doesn't mean adding more layers of helpdesk tickets. It means embedding champions within business units, offering just-in-time guidance, and building up literacy over time.

Data accountability is a living system. It touches roles, processes, incentives, and culture. The organizations that get this right don't treat data as an abstract asset managed by IT. They treat it as a shared resource, governed with discipline and owned with pride.

Privacy, Security, and Responsible Access

Data only delivers value when it is trusted. That trust is not earned through accuracy alone; it stems from protection. In today's hyper-connected world, data underpins customer relationships, employee confidence, and organizational integrity. This makes data security and privacy both a technical responsibility and a strategic priority.

To lead effectively in this environment, leaders must cultivate stewardship. That begins with a mindset shift: treating privacy and protection not as barriers to innovation but as the conditions that allow it to flourish. When customers believe their information is handled responsibly and employees trust the systems around them, momentum accelerates. Innovation can't thrive in an atmosphere of hesitation.

The first act of stewardship is restraint. Collecting excess data "just in case" increases risk without increasing value. The more information stored, the greater the exposure. A responsible approach starts by defining the minimum viable dataset required for each customer interaction or internal process. Anything more becomes a liability, expanding the target surface for misuse or breach.

This is especially urgent in regulated industries. Legal frameworks such as the GDPR and the Health Insurance Portability and Accountability Act exist to protect people from misuse of their most personal information. For companies operating globally or handling sensitive health, financial, or identity-related data, these mandates are foundational safeguards of public trust.

Leaders should begin by classifying data according to sensitivity. Not all data carries equal risk, but treating all data the same dilutes focus. Personally identifiable information such as names, addresses, payment credentials, or health records requires encryption both at rest and in transit, as well as tightly controlled access rights. Without these safeguards, exposure risk multiplies.

Yet most breaches do not come from external hackers. They originate from within through misconfigurations, accidental disclosures, or malicious behavior by insiders. According to Verizon's *Data Breach Investigations Report*, over 74 percent of data breaches involve the human element, including privilege misuse and simple errors.[16] This reality underscores the need for layered defenses. Start with strong identity authentication, role-based access controls, and data masking. Where possible, use anonymized or synthetic datasets for AI model training to avoid exposing real identities during testing.

Security also demands cultural clarity. Every employee, from engineer to executive, must understand their role in safeguarding data. This requires embedding protection into the company's values and operating rhythms. When pressures rise, corner-cutting becomes tempting. But trust, once lost, is not easily restored.

---

16   *2024 Data Breach Investigations Report* (Verizon Business, 2024), https://www.verizon.com/business/resources/Tdd9/reports/2024-dbir-data-breach-investigations-report.pdf.

Governance mechanisms should evolve with the business. Just as systems are stress-tested and performance is measured, data protections require regular auditing. Leaders should ask: Where are the biggest risks? Who has access? What happens if sensitive data ends up in the wrong hands? These are not IT questions; they are business questions.

As AI systems scale, new risks emerge. A model trained on unprotected data may unintentionally recreate or reveal sensitive inputs. That's why synthetic data structured to reflect real-world patterns without exposing personal details has become essential. It enables teams to experiment and innovate safely.

We often refer to data as an asset. But like any asset, it retains its value only when handled with care. In a world where trust is hard-earned and easily lost, how you protect data may be the clearest reflection of your values and your readiness to lead.

Creating a Data-First Culture

If the first half of the data journey is about infrastructure—what you collect, how you store it, and how you protect it—the second half is about behavior. No matter how advanced your architecture or polished your dashboards, if your people don't trust the data or know how to use it, transformation stalls. Building a data-first culture requires a mindset shift. And it has to start at the top.

If the executive team makes decisions based on gut instinct while the rest of the organization is told to follow the numbers, a double standard forms. That creates confusion and kills momentum. A true data-first culture doesn't reject intuition, but it doesn't elevate it above evidence either. Experience should inform hypotheses, not serve as the final word. And the only way to change that dynamic is to model the behavior you expect from others.

That means consistently asking questions grounded in the data. What does the information say about this trend? How confident are we in these numbers? Do we have the full picture or are we acting on fragments? The more often leaders ask these questions in rooms where decisions are being made, the more it signals that data matters, not just as a technical layer but as the foundation for clear thinking and confident execution.

But even the best intent can be undermined by organizational habits. When every team builds its own spreadsheet, when key metrics have multiple versions, when debates hinge on whose number is "more right," it's a sign that data trust is broken. And that's not just a systems problem. It's a cultural one. When people don't trust the official systems, they work around them. They create local versions. They pull reports, clean them by hand, and make small adjustments "just to get what I need." That might seem harmless in the moment, but it creates divergence—different teams working from different truths, with no consistent way to align, measure, or improve.

Fixing this starts with shared ownership. Data is not the responsibility of a single team buried in IT or operations. It's an organizational asset. Everyone who touches data—collects it, enters it, cleans it, or analyzes it—plays a role in its integrity. Leaders must make clear that every team is a data steward. And the only way to maintain trust in the system is to treat data with care at every stage.

That also means simplifying how data is presented. If your frontline teams have to decode cryptic dashboards or wade through dense reports to find what matters, they won't use the data. They'll go back to what they know—intuition, anecdotes, and "the way we've always done it." Data that overwhelms or confuses becomes noise.

And noise is the enemy of confidence. The most powerful insights are the ones that are clear, accessible, and directly tied to the goals teams are trying to achieve.

Simplicity is not dumbing things down but finding clarity. When a sales manager sees a simple scorecard that shows how their region is performing against personalized offers, they know exactly what to focus on. When a product owner sees engagement drop-offs at a specific point in the customer journey, they can pinpoint what needs to change.

And then there's storytelling. This might be one of the most underrated tools in culture change. When one team uncovers a valuable insight that drives real impact, that story should be shared widely. It's not just about celebrating a win. It's about showing what's possible. How did they frame the problem? What data did they use? What changed as a result? These stories create social proof. They show that the data isn't just theoretical. It's practical. It works. And it's making a difference.

Over time, those stories add up. They start to shift the way people talk about data while reducing fear. And they encourage others to look for their own insights. That's how you move from isolated use cases to cultural adoption, with data becoming part of how decisions get made, not just a report someone runs once a month.

Of course, none of this happens overnight. Culture change is hard. It requires consistency, reinforcement, and sometimes uncomfortable conversations. But the signals are always there. If you're seeing conflicting metrics, shadow systems, or decisions made without evidence, it's time to look beyond the tools and examine the behavior.

AVOIDING DATA QUALITY PITFALLS IN AI PROJECTS

Many companies encounter costly traps when starting AI initiatives, often driven by excitement and high hopes but lacking a deep understanding of their data. Here are some key pitfalls to watch out for:

- Assuming data is ready: Underestimating the effort needed to clean and organize data can cause significant delays.

- Prioritizing models over data: Advanced AI models depend on quality data. Even simple models can outperform complex ones if trained on better data.

- Letting bias influence AI: Biased training data will produce biased results, risking harm to individuals and damaging your organization's reputation.

- Expecting data problems to fix themselves: Getting new tools or hiring experts won't instantly solve data issues. Thorough data preparation is crucial.

- Ignoring fairness: Biased datasets lead to unfair AI decisions, causing problems in hiring, lending, healthcare, and more while also reducing public trust.

- Overlooking data governance: Clear rules about data ownership and quality are essential. Poor governance results in unreliable data and wasted effort.

- Scaling before the data is ready: Don't grow your AI projects until your data is clean, unbiased, and well managed, or you may amplify existing issues.

The key lesson here is that by avoiding these pitfalls and focusing on data quality, you'll save resources, protect your reputation, and stay compliant, building a solid foundation for your AI efforts.

How Leaders Measure Data's Real Impact

At the end of the day, every data initiative comes down to one question: Was the juice worth the squeeze? It's a fair ask. You've invested the time, restructured teams, upgraded systems, built new dashboards, and trained people to think differently. The natural next step is to look around and ask, What changed? What improved? And how do we know?

The trap leaders fall into is equating activity with impact. Reports get built. Dashboards light up. There's no shortage of numbers. But if those numbers don't shape decisions, influence behavior, or move the needle on real business outcomes, then you're measuring the wrong things. The goal isn't to prove how much data you have; it's to show what it helped you do better.

The most effective way to measure impact is to track a small set of high-level metrics that align with your strategic goals. Start by identifying three to five outcomes that your data efforts are meant to influence. That could be improving customer retention, boosting sales in a specific segment, reducing operational costs, or speeding up time to market. If your data strategy isn't contributing to one or more of those outcomes, then you have a strategy problem, not a reporting problem.

These metrics don't belong in a dense report buried at the bottom of an email thread. They should be visible, executive-friendly, and updated regularly. You want a scorecard that makes it easy to see where progress is happening and where attention is needed. That means ditching the complex analytics language and surfacing insight in plain English. What changed? Why did it change? What action are we taking because of it?

There's power in simplicity. A scorecard that shows churn dropped 8 percent after a personalized outreach campaign tied to better segmentation is far more compelling than a chart with forty-seven attributes and a regression curve no one can explain.

That's where trust becomes nonnegotiable, especially as predictive models and AI systems become more embedded in day-to-day operations. It's not enough for a model to make a call. Leaders want to know how it made the call. What variables were weighed? What signals mattered most? Was the decision fair, accurate, and consistent? The value of data is only as strong as the confidence leaders have in the story it tells and their willingness to act on it.

The value of data is only as strong as the confidence leaders have in the story it tells and their willingness to act on it.

Now, explainability shifts from a technical concept to a business imperative. If a model flags a customer as likely to churn, a leader should understand why. Did their engagement drop? Did their support experience suffer? Did their purchase patterns shift? That transparency builds trust. And that trust becomes the foundation for broader adoption across the organization.

When you tie those predictions to real-world impact—lower attrition, higher conversion rates, better demand forecasting—you start to build a pattern of proof. And that pattern is what drives confidence in the data journey as a whole. Not just because the model said so, but because it delivered meaningful results that could be validated.

Another signal of maturity is how quickly and confidently teams can act on insight. If your dashboards are full of interesting facts but decisions are still made the old-fashioned way—based on hierarchy, hunches, or who speaks loudest in the room—you've got a culture issue. Real value shows up in how data accelerates cycles. Faster answers. Better coordination. More precise adjustments. Less time lost debating whose number is right.

This is why regular business impact reviews are essential. Schedule them. Make them standard. Use them to ask simple, powerful questions. What decisions did we make because of the data? What worked? What didn't? What did we learn? And what's next?

Don't stop at the output. Focus on the outcome. If the new data pipeline helped reduce shipping errors, what was the cost savings? If automated forecasting improved inventory planning, how did that affect margins? If the customer experience became more personalized, did satisfaction scores go up? Did conversion rates improve? Did churn slow down?

That's where you start to see the real return. It's about velocity and value. How quickly can you turn data into insight? And how reliably can you translate that insight into action that matters?

When you start to build success stories into your operating rhythm, the culture shifts. Teams stop asking, Why are we doing this? and start asking, What else can we improve? That's when you know the juice was worth the squeeze. And that's how data moves from a technical initiative to a strategic advantage.

FIVE STEPS TO TAKE NOW

Building a data-driven organization begins with trust. To scale AI, automation, and intelligent decision-making, you need a data foundation that is consistent, complete, and confidently used by your teams. These five steps will help you move from insight to action, turning your data into a strategic advantage.

Step 1: Conduct a Data Confidence Pulse Check

Ask five leaders across your organization to answer one deceptively simple question: *How many active customers do we have this month?* Listen not just for the number but for how quickly and confidently they answer, and whether they all say the same thing. If they hesitate, disagree, or check with someone, you've uncovered a trust gap. Use that gap to spark a wider audit of key metrics: Where do definitions drift? Where are manual workarounds replacing official systems? What data is consistently questioned or ignored?

Step 2: Appoint a Data Owner for Every Critical Domain

Every major data domain—customer, product, financials, inventory—needs a named owner. This isn't an honorary title. It's an accountability structure. Data owners define what *clean* means, set validation rules, ensure definitions are consistent across systems, and have the authority to escalate fixes when needed. Without ownership, data decays. With it, teams have a steward who protects quality and champions clarity. Start by mapping your core domains, identifying existing gaps, and assigning responsibility that aligns to business needs.

Step 3: Run a Cross-Functional Data Friction Sprint

Bring together leaders from marketing, operations, finance, IT, and customer service. Ask each team to surface two places where data slows them down, whether because of inaccuracy, inaccessibility, or inconsistency. Chart the ripple effects across departments. Then, identify one area where a fix would unlock broad momentum. Whether it's unifying customer IDs, standardizing product codes, or reconciling sales definitions, address it as a team. One visible win builds confidence and fuels cultural change.

Step 4: Evaluate Explainability in One Key AI or Analytics System

Choose one high-impact model or dashboard your organization uses regularly. Ask three essential questions:

- What data drives its recommendations?
- Can a business leader explain how it works to their team?
- Who is accountable for its outputs?

If answers are vague, it's time to clarify. Build a basic explainer, assign an owner, and flag any black-box risks. Explainability is a gateway to broader adoption, trust, and smarter decision-making.

Step 5: Share One Story That Proves the Data Works

Find one team that used data to improve outcomes, whether it was reduced churn, better inventory planning, or faster onboarding. Document what they did, what they learned, and what changed. Then share that story widely in all-hands meetings, newsletters, or one-on-ones. This builds social proof and shows teams what's possible. Highlight the behavior, not just the result. The more you show how insight leads to action, the more others will want to follow suit.

The real power of data isn't in its volume; it's in its ability to accelerate trust, action, and transformation. One disciplined step at a time is how you turn your data from a liability into lasting leverage.

PART IV

DIRECTING THE CHANGE

CHAPTER EIGHT

IDENTIFYING NEW BUSINESS MODELS

*The real voyage of discovery consists not in seeking
new landscapes but in having new eyes.*

—MARCEL PROUST

> **Your Mission Possible Blueprint:** You can't build the future
> by protecting the past. And you can't unlock new value by
> optimizing old assumptions. This chapter is your blueprint for
> identifying, testing, and scaling business models that match
> the pace, complexity, and individuality of today's customer.
> You'll walk away with a strategic framework for rethinking
> how your business creates and delivers value—from internal
> friction that hides untapped potential to platform models
> that scale relevance with speed.

WHEN WE TALK about business model innovation, the conversation often defaults to companies such as Amazon, Apple, or Netflix.

Their names have become shorthand for disruption and success. But modeling their surface-level strategies misses the deeper point. The goal isn't to replicate the giants. It's to absorb the boldness behind their choices, the mindset that allowed them to rethink what was possible and build entirely new ways to deliver value.

The iPhone wasn't just a better phone. It redefined what a phone *was* and turned it into the foundation for a new digital ecosystem. AWS didn't simply offer cloud storage. It unlocked a new era of scalable digital infrastructure, giving startups the power to operate like enterprises and enterprises the agility to move like startups. These weren't just product launches. They were platform shifts. They reimagined the model altogether.

True innovation lives in reframing the question itself. Too often, businesses chase improvement when what's required is reinvention. Take the old adage about building a better mousetrap. For years, that meant refining the spring, adjusting the bait, or modifying the mechanism. Disruption, on the other hand, reimagines the entire concept of pest control. Maybe it prevents mice from entering in the first place. Maybe it repels them without harm. Maybe it reimagines the entire ecosystem that made the problem relevant.

> *Too often, businesses chase improvement when what's required is reinvention.*

Business model innovation starts by asking different questions through a MEx lens. What if the entire journey could be rebuilt to remove friction, accelerate decisions, and deepen loyalty? What if the value a customer receives isn't defined by the product alone but by the experience wrapped around it? These MEx-driven questions are the foundation for the next era of growth.

This is where ME x ME enters the frame as a design principle. At its core, it combines two powerful forces: personalization for the individual and scale for the enterprise. This is the intersection where modern business models are born. The ME customer doesn't want to browse dozens of irrelevant options. They want immediate relevance, predictive service, and seamless resolution. They want to feel seen, heard, and valued in every interaction, across every channel, without repetition or delay. And the second ME? That's your company, reflecting a clear, data-driven understanding of each individual's needs. Together, these two forces form a multiplying effect. One amplifies the other. That's the power behind ME x ME.

ME x ME FRAMEWORK

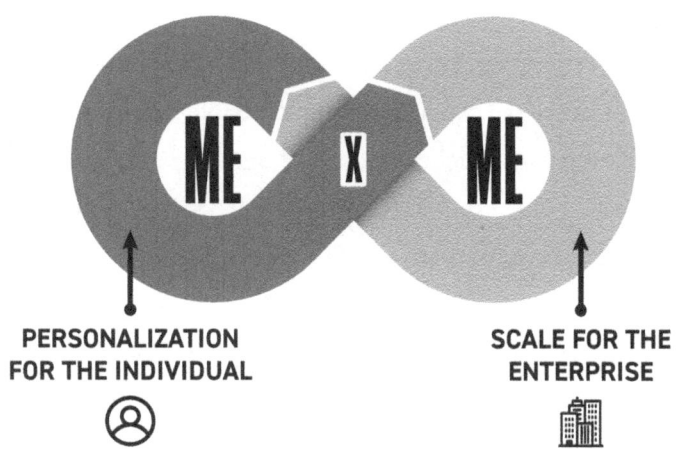

Today's most transformational business models go beyond delivering products or services more efficiently. They collapse complexity and remove decision fatigue. They give time back to customers by removing steps, automating workflows, and personalizing outcomes. And they challenge the belief that innovation belongs solely to tech companies or venture-backed startups. In reality, any company, regardless of industry, can architect new models of value when they embrace this lens.

Imagine what this looks like in practice. A traditional travel site presents endless filters, hotel listings, and car rental options. It hands the work to the user. Now contrast that with a conversational experience driven by intelligent technology. You simply explain to an AI-generated avatar where you want to go, what you like to eat, the pace you prefer, your budget, and your goals for the trip. It will ask intuitive questions, and within minutes, a fully built itinerary will be presented, reservations included, language preferences honored, and schedule optimized. The entire model shifts from self-navigation to guided curation. This exemplifies MEx in action—hyperpersonalized outcomes for the individual traveler (ME) delivered through scalable, data-driven systems (enterprise capability).

Retailers are doing the same. Instead of asking customers to browse endless pages, immersive experiences allow people to model their own living rooms; swap out couches, rugs, and lighting; and walk through their future space before they buy. By creating an experience, retailers have minimized returns, boosted satisfaction, and unlocked confidence. The business model now revolves around personal immersion and digital confidence as opposed to showroom square footage.

When leaders start to view innovation through this lens, something changes. The ambition gets clearer. The questions get sharper. They stop asking, How can we improve what we have? and start asking, What would this look like if we built it from scratch, using everything we now know about our customer, our data, and our capabilities?

But this kind of shift requires courage. It asks leaders to let go of legacy mental models and embrace a blank-page approach. It calls for partnerships across functions, faster experimentation cycles, and a deep commitment to data-informed decision-making. But the reward is massive. Business models built on this foundation are more resilient, more scalable, and more attuned to what customers actually want instead of what companies *assume* they want.

Innovation, at its highest level, is not a function or a lab or a once-a-year offsite. It's a fundamental rethinking of how value is created, delivered, and experienced.

Reinventing from Within

Before AWS became the backbone of the modern internet, powering everything from scrappy startups to Fortune 100 enterprises, it was simply Amazon's solution to its own growing complexity. That's the part of the story often overlooked. AWS didn't start with a plan to disrupt the infrastructure market. It started with a simple problem: Internal teams couldn't move fast enough. Every new product, every new service, required the same repetitive infrastructure work—provisioning servers, configuring storage, and establishing access protocols. The development pipeline was clogged, innovation was slowing, and talented engineers were spending their time reinventing the same wheel.

So the question was asked: What if we broke the infrastructure down into reusable building blocks? What if we built a common set of internal services—storage, compute, databases—that any team could access on demand, without needing to start from scratch? That simple shift in mindset changed everything. What began as an effort to reduce friction internally became one of the most significant technology platforms of the last two decades. AWS wasn't born as a commercial product. It emerged as an answer to the complexity that was stalling Amazon's own teams. The decision to externalize it, turning internal plumbing into external value, was a natural next step.

This is the quiet power of looking inward. Often, the next frontier of market innovation is hiding in the friction you're already tolerating. The broken handoffs. The duplicated work. The tools your teams keep duct-taping together to make things function. When approached with intention, these nuisances reveal the opportunity to reframe inefficiency as innovation.

This is where the concept of thinking in primitives becomes a game-changer. Instead of viewing your systems and processes as monolithic entities, break them down into their elemental components—the smallest usable parts that can be reused, recombined, and extended. It's the same way software engineering evolved. Instead of hardcoded functionality, we moved toward APIs, microservices, and reusable libraries. Each primitive becomes a service, and each service can power not just one solution, but many.

The genius of AWS wasn't that it provided servers in the cloud. It was that it turned infrastructure into a set of composable, on-demand services that developers could consume like utilities. It moved from building products to enabling ecosystems. And in doing so, it unlocked exponential scale. Developers didn't have to ask permission. They just built a solution quickly, cheaply, and at massive scale.

This is a lesson every leader can apply. Start by identifying the pain points that keep surfacing inside your own organization. Where are teams slowed down? Where do customers get frustrated? Where do the same workarounds show up again and again? These are more than just problems to fix. They may be platforms waiting to be born.

This shift in thinking requires a new lens. Stop asking what you can build *for* the market and start asking what you've already built *inside* that might be valuable *to* the market. Ask where your internal strengths could become modular services. What's invisible today that, if surfaced and structured, could become a competitive advantage?

Traditional companies build and sell finished products. Modern platform companies create systems that others can build on. They empower innovation in others. That's the difference between selling a solution and enabling a movement.

Platform thinking embodies "everybody wins" at scale. Customers access personalized experiences tailored to their needs. Third-party partners reach new markets and capabilities they couldn't build alone. The platform operator captures value by making others successful—growth becomes mutual rather than zero-sum.

This mindset applies far beyond technology. Think about service models, training programs, even governance frameworks. A financial services firm, for example, might develop a robust internal process for validating AI-driven recommendations. Instead of keeping that process locked inside, they could structure it as a transparent, modular framework, enabling clients to understand, trust, and extend the models they use. That builds confidence, drives adoption, and creates loyalty through openness.

Reinvention doesn't always require a clean slate. Often, it means surfacing and refining what's already in motion and recognizing that internal excellence can become external value if you structure it, standardize it, and give it room to scale.

Why Speed and Imperfection Are Strategic Assets

The first version of AWS wasn't elegant or polished. And it certainly wasn't built to support the digital infrastructure of the global economy. But it did one thing exceptionally well: *It worked.* It solved an internal problem, it provided clear value, and it gave teams a chance to build something new without waiting for permission. That was enough. Because the goal wasn't perfection but *learning*.

This is one of the most important lessons in building for the future: Version one (V1) doesn't need to be flawless. It needs to be useful. Waiting for perfection is how great ideas die in PowerPoint decks and project reviews. The real progress begins when a customer, internal or external, can touch something and say, "That's better than what I had before."

This is one of the most important lessons in building for the future: Version one (V1) doesn't need to be flawless. It needs to be useful.

Leaders today must embrace a mindset of continuous iteration. In a world where technology changes weekly and customer expectations shift with every new digital experience, the best strategy is often momentum. Not recklessness, but focused, intentional motion. The ability to move fast, respond to real-world feedback, and course-correct quickly is a strategic imperative.

At Amazon, this idea is embedded in the culture as a bias for action. It reflects a simple but powerful belief: Speed matters. When an opportunity presents itself, it won't wait for a ten-step approval process. Customers won't wait for an internal alignment memo. And innovation won't happen on your timeline. It happens when the conditions are right and when someone is willing to go first. That's what having a bias for action really means: being willing to test, to fail, to learn, and to try again—faster than the competition.

But moving fast means launching with a clear hypothesis and using every interaction as a source of insight. This is why experimentation, not prediction, becomes the engine of growth. It's the difference between writing a business case filled with assumptions and designing a prototype that exposes what's true. When you test early and often, the market tells you what matters. Real customers show you what works. That feedback is your compass.

The original AWS teams didn't know they were creating the most successful cloud platform in history. They thought they were trying to unblock developers. The first version of S3 made storing and retrieving objects easier. Then they listened. They learned. And they layered in capabilities based on what users actually needed, not what they assumed would be impressive in a press release. That discipline of building around real-world constraints is what allowed AWS to scale with such precision.

This is the kind of thinking leaders must adopt when navigating transformation. Instead of overoptimizing for theoretical outcomes, focus on delivering something small that's actually valuable. Start with the problem. Launch the simplest version that addresses it. Then use *that* as the foundation for learning.

This also means rethinking how success is measured. Too often, initiatives are judged by their polish instead of their progress. Leaders should reward learning velocity, that is, how quickly and constructively a team can generate insight and use it to improve. A failed prototype that reveals a better customer need is worth more than a beautiful solution that solves the wrong problem.

A failed prototype that reveals a better customer need is worth more than a beautiful solution that solves the wrong problem.

Iteration also requires a shift in how we think about risk. The biggest risk today is in moving too slow, not too fast. Markets change and competitors evolve. The organizations that win aren't the ones that make the fewest mistakes. They're the ones that recover fastest and evolve with purpose.

This plays directly into the principle of building for the customer you have, not the one you imagine. Every time you iterate, you learn something new about your actual users—their habits, their pain points, and their preferences. You move beyond personas and assumptions into patterns and truths. You stop designing for idealized users and start delivering for real ones. That's where real loyalty is built.

This is also why V1 thinking matters so much. When you commit to getting V1 into the world quickly, you give your teams permission to try. You lower the stakes and reduce the fear of failure. And most importantly, you create momentum. Nothing inspires progress like a working solution, even if it's imperfect. Once it exists, people can see it, touch it, and react to it. They can suggest improvements and imagine new use cases. But none of that happens until something ships.

So the challenge for leaders is simple: Create an environment where progress is possible. Because in a world where the future is being built one experiment at a time, the organizations that thrive will be the ones that never stop learning and never wait for perfect.

Customer Obsession as a Business Model Strategy

Amazon's day one mindset reflects a commitment to staying close to the evolving needs of MEx. It informs decisions not only during the launch of a product but throughout its entire lifecycle. This approach sustains relevance by embedding the customer's experience into the way the business operates and grows. When a business model is rooted in that level of awareness, it becomes inherently more adaptable and resilient.

The original impact of AWS stemmed from the clarity of the problem it addressed. Developers were spending disproportionate time managing infrastructure rather than building. Teams faced delays from procurement cycles, restrictive processes, and growing complexity. The value AWS delivered came from creating a system that reduced that operational burden. It enabled flexibility, responsiveness, and scale by design. The solution itself was grounded in the practical friction internal teams encountered every day. That friction was shared by developers globally, and AWS became the model that answered it.

This is where customer obsession becomes operational. Listening becomes an active process, one that extends beyond formal feedback channels. Customers express their needs in how they behave: where they hesitate, what they abandon, which tools they gravitate toward, and which processes they avoid. These behaviors create a pattern of unmet needs, often long before those needs are verbalized.

Strategic insight often lives in subtle patterns. Extended dwell time on a single page, repeated exits from a checkout flow, or unusual usage of a particular feature each offers a signal. The organizations that tune in to these signals with discipline are the ones that learn faster and evolve with greater precision. Their systems interpret the signals in ways that translate into improvement.

The business models that last tend to be built on this habit of continuous listening. When customer interaction is treated as a learning event, the business builds in mechanisms for course correction and reinvention. Momentum comes not from a single moment of insight but from the consistent practice of observing where MEx expectations fall short and where improvements can be made.

Listening at this level requires a different kind of leadership. It rewards curiosity and reinforces the value of staying attuned to shifting patterns. When leaders remain focused on what people are trying to achieve rather than what the product was originally designed to do, they stay closer to the next opportunity. This kind of proximity to the problem creates clarity around what matters most.

Of course, listening is only the first step. The organizations that pull furthest ahead are those that use what they hear to anticipate needs before customers even voice them—building proactive, AI-powered experiences that create lasting competitive advantage. We'll explore exactly how they do this in the next chapter, but it is this listening-driven approach to customer-centered innovation that shapes pricing models, service delivery, support systems, and business infrastructure. AWS introduced consumption-based billing, global redundancy, and self-service provisioning, all of which addressed long-standing constraints developers had learned to work around. These changes reshaped expectations about how infrastructure could be consumed.

This dynamic is playing out across other industries as well. In retail, virtual try-on tools reduce the uncertainty customers feel when shopping for clothing or furniture. These tools might feel like a novelty, but they solve for confidence and accuracy at the point of decision. In financial services, AI-driven guidance gives customers clarity in moments that previously felt ambiguous. The impact is measured in confidence, loyalty, and better outcomes.

Organizations that prioritize this kind of design are often the ones that stay closest to the real-world complexity their customers navigate. They study the entire journey and surface the pain points people have quietly adapted to. And they respond by removing friction with intention and care.

Customer obsession, as a strategic principle, produces results that accumulate. Trust increases. Engagement deepens. Loyalty follows. And because each improvement is based on behavior, the system stays in motion without losing direction. Customers will pay or consume or try something more readily if they see value in successful use with it. Did it save time? Did it simplify or solve a major problem? Does it meld well with the way their business operates or open new ways for the business to operate? Is it easy to try, easy to buy, and easy to use? Can the customer create their own internal competitive moat by using the solution? All of these questions represent different ways of satisfying MEx, but all are based on MEx gaining value.

The Hidden Levers of Growth

Some of the most transformative innovations in business begin with decisions that appear to challenge conventional logic. These are the moments that stretch a company's comfort zone and force it to reconsider how success is defined. What often looks like a risky move from the outside is, in practice, a calculated choice rooted in a deeper understanding of value creation. I call these strategies *anti-patterns*. They run counter to accepted norms but often become the very levers that unlock outsized growth.

At the launch of AWS, Amazon's developers were bogged down by repetitive infrastructure tasks. The systems they relied on were inconsistent, fragmented, and time-consuming. They built new tools not as an experiment but because they had no choice. In solving for their own inefficiencies, they created something far more scalable: a platform that could support others navigating similar challenges.

The pivotal moment came when Amazon chose to make these internal capabilities externally available. The very infrastructure that powered Amazon's core business was opened up to the market, including to companies that would eventually become direct competitors. This was a strategic investment in future relevance. By producing its internal tools and turning them into a platform, Amazon created a new growth engine that would fuel long-term innovation across the company.

Moves like this rarely feel comfortable in the moment. They ask leaders to examine their most valuable systems and consider whether those systems should evolve into something different—something that might serve others, even those outside the traditional ecosystem. It requires a level of clarity about where advantage comes from and a willingness to shift that advantage to create something larger.

Legacy systems and existing profit centers often slow this kind of thinking. When a business has achieved success through a particular model, that model becomes protected. Processes become locked in, and teams build careers around defending the familiar. Leaders begin to prioritize predictability over progress. But disruption rarely waits for permission. It moves quickly, and often through the paths that legacy organizations choose to ignore.

What distinguishes companies that stay relevant is their ability to act before change is forced upon them. They evaluate their current strengths not as endpoints but as raw material for what comes next. When those strengths begin to slow progress, they are reimagined and redeployed in ways that create new forms of value. This is the essence of self-disruption. It's a form of stewardship, guided by foresight and informed by responsibility to the future.

Inside these organizations, innovation becomes a behavior modeled at every level. Leaders support teams that challenge assumptions and pursue ideas that may seem uncomfortable at first. They create space for experimentation, build feedback mechanisms that expose blind spots, and reward initiative over adherence. This cultural permission is often what separates bold decisions from theoretical strategies.

*Cultural permission is often what separates
bold decisions from theoretical strategies.*

Anti-patterns, which are contrarian strategies that oftentimes prove to be better than following the herd, appear across industries, often just before an inflection point. A media company may choose to prioritize community over ad impressions. A retailer might lean into third-party marketplaces to expand reach. A software provider could open-source its core tools to accelerate adoption, knowing that growth will follow from engagement rather than exclusivity. Each of these choices reflects a shift in mindset: from guarding the current advantage to building the next one.

The companies that lead through disruption tend to recognize change as an opportunity rather than a threat. They focus on designing future-facing models that align with emerging behavior, unmet needs, and new forms of value creation. This orientation allows them to adapt with speed and scale with confidence.

Growth, in this context, becomes less about iteration and more about reframing the fundamentals. Retiring a profitable product may clear the way for a more sustainable model. Supporting a new initiative that competes with an existing offering can sharpen focus and accelerate differentiation. These decisions require clarity of intent and the conviction to act in service of long-term health, even when short-term certainty is tempting.

The discomfort that often accompanies these moments is a marker of proximity to meaningful change. When existing systems begin to feel strained, when legacy processes start to slow innovation, and when competitors are building on infrastructure you helped define, those signals point to a deeper opportunity: the chance to lead again, this time from a renewed position of strength.

Worlds, Not Screens

The internet is entering a new era—one defined not by screens and scrolls but by presence. We are moving from observing digital content to inhabiting it. This shift transforms how people engage with information, make decisions, and connect with brands from a sensory perspective. It calls for a fundamental rethinking of business design. The immersive internet is the next layer of infrastructure.

At the heart of this transformation is the rise of fully personalized environments. We've moved beyond recommendation engines and curated product feeds. Today's customers expect entire experiences to respond to their context, preferences, and intent. The emerging standard is where customers no longer want to click through static options. They want to step into worlds that understand them.

This is where immersive technologies—augmented reality, virtual reality, spatial computing—become essential. These tools are becoming the default infrastructure for how products are explored, services are delivered, and decisions are made. A static product grid may inform. But a dynamic virtual experience builds trust. It allows people to try, compare, and commit in ways that feel intuitive, confident, and even creative. Think of an avatar of Gordon Ramsay, for instance, at a store—helping you pick a recipe, telling you where to find all of the ingredients, and interacting with you in a conversational way, the way humans think, learn, and communicate. Couple that with MEx personalization, and it's a game-changer.

Or consider the travel industry. Planning a trip has traditionally meant juggling multiple platforms, tabs, and reviews. It's a task that requires constant translation between options and personal preferences. Now imagine interacting with an AI-powered assistant that understands your constraints, curates your itinerary, walks you through the sights, previews accommodations in immersive settings, and books everything in one seamless conversation. No switching between systems. No guesswork. Just clarity and momentum.

These experiences are already possible with the technology available today. What's changing is the mindset required to build them. When immersive interactions are treated as central to the business model rather than side projects, they begin to reshape how value is created. Immersion reduces the gap between curiosity and commitment. It shortens the path from "I'm interested" to "I'm in."

This dynamic is already playing out in retail. A customer buying a couch no longer needs to imagine how it will look in their space. With a smartphone, they can scan the room, place the item at scale, rotate it, try different fabrics, and decide within minutes—all without leaving home. That experience eliminates friction and increases confidence. And it turns consideration into action to buy.

Fashion brands are creating similar shifts. With virtual try-ons, customers can see how clothes move with their body type, explore accessory combinations, and make decisions that reflect how they want to look and feel. In automotive, buyers can explore vehicle interiors, toggle features, and take immersive test drives, all before setting foot in a dealership. These are not enhanced versions of old processes but entirely new experiences that reframe how people buy.

The real value of immersion lies in its ability to reduce cognitive effort. When customers don't have to imagine or translate abstract information, they engage more deeply. Their decisions become faster and more confident. And those interactions build emotional memory, the kind of connection that drives long-term loyalty.

When customers don't have to imagine or translate abstract information, they engage more deeply. Their decisions become faster and more confident.

To build this kind of engagement, leaders need to treat immersive technology as part of core business design, not as an optional innovation layer. They need to reimagine high-friction interactions and turn them into seamless, intuitive, emotionally resonant environments. Every moment of hesitation, every time a customer wonders if the product will fit, if the service will work, or if the price is worth it, is an invitation to redesign the experience around confidence.

Immersive business models also unlock a new scale of flexibility. Digital showrooms and virtual inventory allow companies to display limitless product combinations without expanding physical space. Teams can serve customers across time zones and geographies without building new storefronts. The business becomes adaptive by design, capable of delivering high-fidelity engagement at scale.

To get there, leaders must start asking a different set of questions. Where are customers still struggling to envision the outcome? Which parts of the journey require too much effort to understand? And how could a reimagined experience bring those moments to life in a way that feels effortless and memorable?

Immersion is emotional interface. It creates a sense of presence and control that static screens cannot replicate. And as the underlying technology becomes more accessible, the barriers to building immersive experiences are falling away quickly. It also potentially opens up new business models and revenue streams. What once required massive investment now takes little more than vision and intent.

Orchestrating the Impossible

The most transformative technologies in business often begin without fanfare. They do not arrive with sweeping announcements or bold predictions. Instead, they enter quietly, folded into existing workflows, solving small problems until, suddenly, they make something possible that once seemed out of reach. Agentic AI is that kind of shift. It does much more than simply speed up isolated tasks. It reframes how entire operations function, moving business forward by turning digital work into a coordinated performance of intelligent systems.

Agentic AI refers to systems that begin with a clear goal and then determine the best path to achieve it. These systems break that goal into discrete steps, arrange those steps in the most effective sequence, execute them across different platforms, and refine their approach based on outcomes. These agents behave more like digital teammates than lines of code, bringing adaptive awareness to the execution of complex work.

Consider a highly specialized consulting firm run by a single expert. With agentic AI, that individual can create an ecosystem of intelligent agents that handle the foundational elements of client engagement. A prospective customer visits the website and interacts with a digital avatar modeled after the consultant. The agent asks questions, captures needs, qualifies the opportunity, drafts a tailored proposal, and schedules the next step. When the consultant joins the conversation, the groundwork is already complete. Human energy is directed at what it does best—creative insight, strategic guidance, and meaningful connection. Everybody wins.

This represents a complete rethinking of how work is structured. To be sure, these agents do not replace the expertise of your team. They amplify it. Much like an engine where small, well-positioned components create massive forward motion, agentic AI links together simple actions to produce complex, high-impact outcomes.

What matters most is not the mechanics of the technology but the space it opens for people to thrive. When machines handle the repeatable work, people recover the time and focus required for higher-order contribution. Instead of being buried in repetitive tasks, they're building relationships, solving nuanced problems, and steering the direction of the business. In this environment, creativity becomes the center of the role. And as a result, customer interactions grow richer and more responsive.

The business impact is layered and compounding. There is a clear reduction in cost as previously manual tasks are executed by systems with minimal oversight. There is a significant gain in speed as processes run continuously without interruption. And there is a powerful lift in personalization, because intelligent agents are capable of processing real-time context at scale.

Take customer onboarding as an example. Traditionally, onboarding involves multiple departments, disconnected tools, and an extended back-and-forth. With agentic AI, one agent can manage the entire workflow. It references previous interactions, gathers missing details, fills out documentation, schedules meetings, and keeps stakeholders informed. The result is a better, shorter onboarding cycle with less friction, greater clarity, and stronger alignment from the start.

The same logic applies to supply chains. Agents can track demand signals, anticipate disruptions, and adjust logistics in real time. In IT, systems can detect issues and deploy fixes before users even notice. In marketing, campaigns can dynamically adjust based on engagement data, reallocating spend and messaging for maximum relevance. In finance, agents can reconcile data, monitor for anomalies, and generate reports with precision. These workflows become living systems, responsive and self-improving.

These tools will continue to shape how forward-looking organizations operate. The question is where leaders are willing to begin. Every organization has routines that drain time and offer little strategic return. These are the processes for which agentic AI delivers the greatest lift. Identifying them is the first step toward building a more intelligent operational backbone.

As you explore these opportunities, boundaries must be set. Agents should operate within clearly defined guardrails. They can complete tasks, escalate exceptions, and log all actions, but they should not be given free rein over financial decisions or legal approvals. Autonomy becomes powerful when paired with visibility and control. It is not the absence of oversight but a new form of accountability.

At the same time, this shift requires leaders to rethink how they allocate human capital. If your most capable employees are spending their time formatting documents or searching for data, their potential is going untapped. Intelligent agents make it possible to reassign that energy to strategy, relationship building, and creative problem-solving—the work that actually moves the business forward.

Agentic AI removes the repetitive noise and elevates the value of human time, bringing clarity to the places where it is best spent.

The Rise of Cognitive AI and Adaptive Intelligence

As intelligent technology continues to evolve, it's becoming increasingly clear that AI cannot be understood as a single category. The early wave of AI systems—those built to recognize images, transcribe speech, or recommend products—delivered extraordinary results within narrow use cases. But these systems remain fixed in scope. They performed the tasks they were built to do without expanding beyond their design. They did not adapt across domains, respond to nuance, or learn dynamically from changing inputs.

Cognitive AI represents a fundamentally different capability. These systems behave less like tools and more like collaborators. They learn from interaction, identify patterns, draw inferences, and adjust their approach based on real-time signals—bringing a level of intelligence that begins to approximate the way people think and respond in unfamiliar situations.

Imagine a professional development platform that doesn't rely on generic training modules but instead acts as a mentor tailored to each individual learner. It understands a person's current role, identifies specific skill gaps, factors in long-term career goals, and considers how that person prefers to learn. It tracks performance as the person progresses, adjusts the pace accordingly, and delivers new resources that align with both individual development and organizational needs. When someone struggles, the system slows down, offers support, and helps the learner work through the challenge.

In onboarding, this kind of intelligence reshapes how people enter a company. A new hire doesn't face a one-size-fits-all experience. Instead, they're guided by an adaptive system that knows their background, understands their role, and suggests specific ways to connect with teams, projects, and priorities. The support offered is contextual and adjusts as the person progresses. It doesn't deliver the same checklist to every employee but rather adapts to the individual and becomes a partner in their growth.

When systems mold themselves to ME rather than asking MEs to mold themselves to systems, it changes the relationship between MEs and the organization. The experience becomes more personal while learning accelerates and engagement deepens. Employees stay because they feel seen, supported, and set up to succeed.

*When systems mold themselves to ME rather than asking
MEs to mold themselves to systems, it changes
the relationship between MEs and the organization.*

Cognitive AI also reshapes the way companies serve customers. A banking application that understands long-term behavior patterns can detect risks before they surface and provide guidance that helps customers stay ahead of financial stress. A wellness platform that monitors subtle changes in sleep patterns, mood, or daily routines can proactively suggest small adjustments that improve well-being before the user is even aware of the decline.

What distinguishes cognitive systems is their ability to grow through use. Each interaction becomes a learning event. With every exchange, the system becomes better at serving the individual. It evolves into a proactive, intelligent service that deepens trust and increases relevance.

To deploy this effectively, leaders must rethink governance. Adaptive systems require a different approach to oversight. You need transparency regarding how the system learns, not to mention clear parameters for ethical alignment. Without this level of visibility, flexibility can become a vulnerability. But when guardrails are strong, and intent is clear, cognitive systems can operate with both creativity and control.

Cognitive AI allows us to deliver handmade experiences at enterprise scale, delivering adaptability without losing accountability. When employees are coached in real time, when customers feel known and supported, and when systems grow more capable the longer they are used, business outcomes improve in every direction.

STRATEGIC FILTERS FOR
PRIORITIZING EMERGING TECH

With new technologies hitting the market every week, it's easy for leaders to feel like they're constantly trying to catch up. The pressure to be ahead of the curve is real. No one wants to be the executive who missed the next big wave. But what often gets missed in the rush is this: You don't need to chase every new tool. You need a strategy that lets the right tools find you.

The companies that lead over time are not the ones that experiment with everything. They're the ones that are ruthlessly intentional—clear about their mission; grounded in the problems they're solving; and disciplined in how they allocate their time, talent, and capital. They have a sharp understanding of what matters most to their customers, their business, and their teams. Technology becomes the amplifier, not the strategy.

That's why we need filters. Not just frameworks for building things once we've chosen them but decision filters to know what's worth our energy in the first place. I use five.

1. Does It Align with a Mission-Critical Problem or Opportunity?

This is the first and most important question. What are the top one or two challenges that, if solved, would move the needle in a meaningful way? What's the one friction point that's limiting customer satisfaction, stalling growth, or costing your team time and resources? If a new technology doesn't map directly to that kind of problem, it might still be interesting, but it doesn't deserve your full attention.

This helps cut through the cool but irrelevant distractions that often creep into innovation pipelines. A great piece of tech without a great problem to solve is just noise. Real business model transformation begins with clarity around what matters.

2. Is It Compatible with Your Current Data Infrastructure?

No matter how impressive the tech, it won't deliver value if it depends on data you don't have or can't trust. Too often, teams try to bolt on the newest AI model or automation tool only to realize their foundational data is fragmented, outdated, or poorly governed.

This isn't a reason to avoid new tools, but it is a reason to evaluate them in context. The right technologies will either align with your current data foundation or create positive pressure to improve it. Either way, they must be part of a coherent data strategy, not an exception to one.

3. Does It Act as a Force Multiplier?

Some technologies just do a new thing. Others make every-thing you already do significantly better. The best ones amplify your strengths, enhance your differentiators, and extend the value of your existing platforms, teams, or processes.

Think of it like compound interest. A force multiplier doesn't add one more capability; it raises the return on everything else you've invested in. Edge computing makes your IoT investments more impactful. Real-time AI analytics make your personalization engines more effective. Look for that kind of synergy.

4. Can It Be Tested with a Small-Scale Experiment?

Leaders don't need certainty to move forward, but they do need a fast feedback loop. The ability to run a contained, low-risk pilot is often what separates a promising idea from an endless debate. Small tests offer real-world data, surface edge cases, and build credibility across teams.

The key here is speed of learning. You're not looking for a polished rollout. You're looking to validate assumptions quickly and use that insight to guide the next decision. A viable experiment is often the simplest signal that a technology is worth exploring further.

5. Is There a Mature and Growing Ecosystem?

No one builds in isolation. Even the best ideas will stall if there's no talent, no tools, and no partner network to support them. That's why I always look at the surrounding ecosystem. Are there platforms you can build on? Are other companies using the technology in production? Are there developers, consultants, or experts who know how to make it work?

Ecosystem maturity accelerates impact. It means you're not building everything from scratch, and you're not taking on the burden of evangelizing something the world hasn't caught up to yet.

When these five filters are used together, they create a powerful lens for strategic focus and ensure that when you say yes, it's to something that truly belongs in your future.

Just as important as what you pursue is what you walk away from. Many organizations burn through time and resources chasing technologies that look good on a slide but never show up where it counts. That's usually because the decision to invest was based on the tool itself rather than the problem it was meant to solve.

Technology should not force you to invent a new strategy just to justify its use. It should fit into the strategy you already have. The strategy built around delivering value, removing friction, serving the customer, and scaling what makes your business special.

The future will always bring new breakthroughs. Your advantage comes not from knowing about them first but from knowing which ones truly belong in your story.

Rapid Prototyping as a Strategic Imperative

Rapid prototyping has often been seen as the domain of product teams or startups. But in today's environment, it needs to be something more. It should be viewed as a leadership behavior, essentially a signal that the organization is capable of thinking quickly, learning continuously, and adjusting with precision. The real question is not whether your company knows how to prototype but whether it's structured to do so with speed, clarity, and intention. When that answer is yes, you're looking at a business built for relevance, not just reliability.

Too often, prototyping is treated like a phase of product development—a task to assign to technical teams once the strategy is set. But in practice, it belongs earlier and higher up in the process. It should shape the conversations happening in boardrooms, influence the priorities reviewed in quarterly planning, and inform the goals tracked in performance dashboards. If your organization is not regularly testing ideas in the market small, fast, and often, then innovation is likely being managed as an abstract ambition rather than a living, active capability.

At the heart of rapid prototyping is the discipline of problem clarity. Every strong prototype begins by clearly defining the user problem. That step sounds simple, but it's where many efforts lose their way. Teams often get excited about a new idea or shiny piece of technology and rush to execution without fully grounding their effort in a specific need. Asking, What are we trying to solve, and for whom? is the filter that separates meaningful innovation from expensive distractions.

Asking, What are we trying to solve, and for whom?
is the filter that separates meaningful innovation
from expensive distractions.

Once the problem is defined, the next move is designing the smallest viable experiment. This isn't a product launch or a refined minimum viable product. It's the fastest, lowest-cost way to generate learning. Can a mock-up get you there? Could a spreadsheet simulate the logic? Would a short email to a few real customers give you the insights you need? The point is to observe how people behave in response to your solution and to refine based on that evidence.

Execution requires small, empowered teams. These teams should be cross-functional, autonomous, and trusted to make decisions as they go. They don't need to operate in isolation, but they do need the ability to move without waiting for approvals at every step. That freedom speeds up the learning loop and makes the organization more responsive to the market. When learning cycles shrink from months to weeks, insight becomes a real-time advantage.

For this to work at scale, teams need success criteria that are clearly defined and tied to outcomes, not output. Did we build it? is the wrong question. Did users engage in the way we hoped? is the better one. A prototype is a test of assumptions. It should generate feedback that sharpens the path forward. Setting the bar in the right place ensures that teams are focused on what matters.

Speed must be balanced with responsibility. This is where governance plays an essential role. Too little structure creates chaos. Too much structure crushes momentum. A smart velocity model addresses both. Teams need to know what types of data are off-limits, what claims require review, and which systems should not be connected without oversight. These boundaries should be explicit and consistent.

Risk tiering is another essential step. Not all experiments carry the same weight. A new app interface and an AI system using customer health data are not equivalent in risk or scrutiny. Defining tiers allows organizations to calibrate the level of governance based on the nature of the work. High-risk efforts get closer review. Low-risk efforts move faster, with lighter oversight.

Decision gates give leadership a structured way to assess progress. These checkpoints are deliberate moments to evaluate whether the prototype is meeting its learning goals and to decide whether to pivot, persevere, or shut it down. This introduces accountability without creating bottlenecks. It also keeps the work aligned with strategic priorities.

Automation plays a role, too. Compliance checks, data scanning, and QA can all be supported by smart tools. Automating those elements reduces manual overhead and ensures that experiments meet consistent standards across the organization. When governance is embedded in the process, it stops being a trade-off with speed.

What makes this approach work is the way it combines creativity with discipline. It gives teams the space to explore while keeping the effort anchored in outcomes that matter. And it builds an organization that knows how to test its assumptions early before risk accumulates and course correction becomes expensive.

Rapid prototyping also reframes failure. In an environment where learning is the goal, a failed experiment is not a loss but rather a decision-making asset. It provides clarity about what does not work, which often becomes the fastest route to discovering what does. The cost of a small test is often insignificant compared to the cost of launching a product that misses the mark.

When prototyping becomes second nature, organizations move with purpose, respond with precision, and learn faster than the competition.

Business Models Built for Motion

Innovation is not a onetime event. It's a system of behavior, repeated, refined, and reinforced at every level of the business. In today's economy, the companies that lead are not simply launching new products. They're building new patterns. They move faster because they learn earlier. They scale smarter because they listen better. And they endure longer because they're willing to change before the market forces them to.

Modern business models are defined by how well they adapt. They translate customer signals into action, transform friction into opportunity, and respond to complexity with clarity. That's what ME x ME makes possible: an operating model designed around individual relevance, delivered at enterprise scale.

The challenge ahead is to move beyond imagining what's possible to building the systems that make it inevitable. That begins with bold questions, fast experiments, intelligent tools, and a deep commitment to serving the customer better than anyone else.

FIVE STEPS TO TAKE NOW

Business model innovation means thinking like a disruptor. There's a lot we couldn't cover in this chapter—you can learn more in The Future Value Field Guide by scanning this QR code and visiting the Insights Hub. But to get you started, these five steps help uncover internal assets, reframe legacy constraints, and identify new ways to create value. The goal is to move from theoretical strategy to executable momentum, one decision at a time.

Step 1: Find Your Platform-in-Waiting

Identify one internal capability—tool, process, or service—that teams consistently rely on but rarely question. Gather a few users and ask:

- What job does this capability actually help us do?
- Where else in the business could it provide value?
- If this were a product, what would it look like?

This shift in lens helps you see operational glue as potential market value.

Step 2: Rethink the Problem Statement

Choose one product, service, or customer journey and rewrite the problem it solves. Push beyond just making it better to ask, What would this look like if it were built for today's customer, using today's tools?

- What behaviors have changed since this model was created?
- Where is complexity causing drop-off, friction, or fatigue?
- What would the ideal experience feel like if we started fresh?

This is your blueprint for reinvention, grounded in relevance rather than legacy.

Step 3: Treat Internal Friction as Market Signal

Document one pain point your teams encounter regularly—manual workarounds, delayed access, or inconsistent tools. Ask:

- Who else outside our walls might face this challenge?
- What data, service, or workflow are we stitching together by force?
- Could this be structured into a reusable solution?

Often, the path to a new business model begins with solving your own problem at scale.

Step 4: Build a V1 with a Real Hypothesis

Identify one capability worth testing with a real audience. Frame the hypothesis clearly:

- Who is this for?
- What outcome will it enable?
- What behavior change would signal success?

Aim for clarity, not polish. A rough but working version is often the fastest way to find out what matters.

Step 5: Run a Reinvention Roundtable

Gather four to six leaders across product, operations, and customer experience. Pose three questions:

- What internal tool or insight have we undervalued?
- Where are we still building for the customer we used to have?
- What small bet could we launch in the next thirty days to explore a new model?

This conversation creates visibility, surfaces opportunity, and accelerates experimentation. Business model transformation starts with business model awareness.

CHAPTER NINE

MODERNIZING EXISTING BUSINESS MODELS AND PROCESSES

If you want something new, you have to stop doing something old.

—PETER F. DRUCKER

Your Mission Possible Blueprint: Modernization starts with a shift in how organizations see, structure, and scale their systems. This chapter is your blueprint for rethinking the core of how work gets done, from the mindsets that shape decisions to the architectures that enable agility. You'll walk away with a practical lens for identifying brittle processes, surfacing hidden costs, and designing new operating models built for change.

THE WORK OF modernization rarely begins with a technology decision. Instead, it begins with a mental model. The most significant transformations I've seen began with a shift in how leaders viewed the business itself. That shift required letting go of long-held assumptions that had quietly calcified into barriers.

One such transformation took place while I was working with a legacy manufacturing company, a firm that had earned its reputation over decades of precision engineering and operational discipline. On paper, they were a model of excellence. Their systems worked and their margins were steady. But the world around them was moving faster. Product cycles were compressing, and customer expectations were fragmenting and multiplying. The demand had shifted from quality to speed, customization, and relevance at scale.

That's when we saw it. What had once made the business great had become the very thing holding it back. The same engineering discipline that delivered predictable excellence had also locked the company into a rigid, sequential way of working. Design handed off to engineering. Engineering handed off to production. Each group operated with deep expertise but in isolation. No one could see the full system end to end, and no one was accountable for how those handoffs actually worked in practice. What they had built was a high-functioning, linear machine, but it couldn't turn. And it certainly couldn't respond to real-time signals from the market.

Modern customers don't wait patiently for a company to catch up. They expect immediacy, relevance, and choice. The MEx economy demands solutions shaped around individual needs and delivered with the same ease and intelligence MEs experience everywhere else in their lives. The company's manufacturing excellence had been optimized for uniformity—one-size-fits-all products delivered through standardized processes. But MEx requires the inverse: customized solutions (ME) delivered through intelligent, flexible systems. The world had moved on, but their business model hadn't.

The MEx economy demands solutions shaped around individual needs and delivered with the same ease and intelligence MEs experience everywhere else in their lives.

The leadership team had been chasing continuous improvement for years. They had implemented new communication tools, upgraded production machinery, and tried to speed up the development pipeline. But every step was still constrained by the original architecture. The faster they tried to go, the more the system strained. Eventually, the cracks showed. A competitor—one less established but far more agile—began outperforming them. From concept to product launch, they moved in one-third the time. And they didn't just ship faster. They adapted in-market, learning from customers as they went. That was the wake-up call.

In one of our early strategy sessions, I remember saying, "You've put a faster engine into a car with a cracked chassis." And that was the moment it clicked. Because when the foundation is brittle, speed only amplifies the fragility. It's like trying to race a car that was never designed for sharp turns. It might perform on a straightaway, but the first disruption sends it spinning off the track.

They realized they needed to step back and rethink the system from the ground up. What would the company look like if it were built today, for today's customers, with today's expectations? That single question changed everything. It moved the conversation from optimization to reimagination.

The shift didn't happen overnight. Legacy systems come with legacy thinking, and unlearning can be harder than learning. But the breakthrough came when the company stopped trying to make the old system faster and started asking what a better system would look like entirely. They had to let go of the idea that their excellence was in how few mistakes they made and begin to explore how quickly they could learn. They had to replace the comfort of specialization with the challenge of shared accountability. And they had to see modernization not as a technology upgrade but as an organizational act of courage.

Legacy systems come with legacy thinking,
and unlearning can be harder than learning.

Unlearning Expertise

One of the most difficult challenges in any modernization effort is convincing a successful organization that change is necessary. High performance creates its own gravity. The more experienced and competent a team becomes at doing things the established way, the harder it becomes to imagine any other way of operating. What begins as mastery eventually becomes a kind of muscle memory, and that muscle memory often turns into resistance. This is the tyranny of the incremental.

When a company consistently hits its numbers—even if just barely—it builds an internal story that says, *What we're doing is working.* And on some level, that's true. The wheels are turning. The product ships. The customers aren't complaining (at least not loudly). In this context, the path of least resistance becomes refinement rather than reinvention. The bias tilts toward lighter lifts, safer bets, and minimal disruption. Leaders are rewarded for making things a little bit better, not for rethinking the system entirely.

But beneath that surface-level stability, something deeper begins to shift. The architecture that holds the business together—its processes, systems, decision rights, and cultural assumptions—starts to show its age. And when change does come, often from outside, it doesn't play by incremental rules. It comes in the form of new competitors who operate with a different blueprint, creating missed opportunities that weren't visible because no one was looking beyond the current model.

Many organizations hide behind agile language while still operating with an incrementalist mindset. They talk about sprints, stand-ups, and minimum viable products, but those rituals don't guarantee transformation. In fact, they can create a false sense of progress. The team is moving, the backlog is shrinking, the demo looks polished, but the business is still solving old problems with old logic. Agile in name alone doesn't change the trajectory. It simply speeds up the loop inside the same constraints.

Many organizations hide behind agile language while still operating with an incrementalist mindset.

The truth is, real modernization is not a UX refresh or a process optimization. It's a systems-level rearchitecture. That means taking a hard look at how the business actually works: where decisions are made, how information flows, what gets prioritized, and how people define success. And it often means inviting discomfort, especially from those who have succeeded under the current model.

That discomfort is where the real work begins. It's the signal that old expertise is being challenged, not discarded. The goal isn't to ignore what has worked in the past but to recontextualize it in light of what's possible *now*. Expertise that refuses to evolve becomes a constraint. But expertise that's willing to unlearn, to ask new questions, and to adopt new mental models becomes a catalyst.

Expertise that refuses to evolve becomes a constraint. But expertise that's willing to unlearn, to ask new questions, and to adopt new mental models becomes a catalyst.

This requires a different type of leadership, not only in vision but in humility. Leaders have to create the conditions for the organization to rethink its habits. Incremental improvements are not inherently wrong. They are essential in many contexts. But when they become the only tool in the strategy toolbox, they create a culture of delay. They postpone the hard decisions and oftentimes mask the deeper issues.

Breaking that cycle begins with the willingness to ask a better question: What if we weren't trying to improve this system but were trying to design a new one entirely?

Mindsets That Scale

Technology can enable change, but mindset is what sustains it. I've seen organizations deploy the latest platforms, rework their architectures, and still fall short because they never updated how they think. Tools can only take you so far if your habits, your assumptions, and your culture are still built around outdated rules. Modernization, at its core, is a leadership mindset shift. And without it, nothing scales.

One of the most important mindset shifts is moving from perfection to learning velocity. In the early days of AWS, every team had the autonomy to launch small experiments to maximize how quickly we could learn from them. Instead of measuring success by how polished a product was, we measured the rate of insight. We learned more in a single quarter of small, iterative experiments than we could have in a year of traditional planning and execution.

Many companies still operate with a perfection mindset, where the safest way to lead is to avoid visible mistakes. But this leads to delay, risk aversion, and a false sense of safety. When progress is measured by how few things go wrong, innovation slows to a crawl. What actually moves the needle is an environment where small failures are studied. When people can test an idea, share what they've learned, and apply it the next time, growth accelerates across the board.

When people can test an idea, share what they've learned, and apply it the next time, growth accelerates across the board.

Another mindset shift involves how authority and action flow through the organization. Traditional models rely on top-down mandates. Leaders define direction. Teams execute. But in fast-moving environments, those layers slow things down. The knowledge required to solve a problem often lives closest to the problem itself. Empowering teams at the edges to act on that knowledge, experiment with solutions, and share results is essential.

I saw this play out firsthand at Microsoft, where Satya Nadella helped the company evolve from a "know-it-all" culture to a "learn-it-all" culture. Leaders were encouraged to ask better questions instead of providing the smartest answers. Teams were given the freedom to explore, to challenge assumptions, and to reshape how value was created. This cultural pivot opened the door to entirely new product categories and market opportunities. Microsoft's renewed agility and customer orientation were the result of a leadership model that invited exploration rather than control.

These shifts don't happen overnight. They require intention and consistency. And perhaps the most transformative shift of all is moving from building gadgets to building platforms. Gadgets solve one problem. Platforms make room for many solutions. A platform mindset is about building for change. It requires modular architecture, API-first thinking, and a willingness to let others contribute, extend, and evolve the system over time.

The real lesson here is about leadership. The role of a modern leader is no longer to dictate direction or possess all the answers. It's to create an environment where the right questions can be asked and better answers can emerge. That means prioritizing learning velocity over perfection, empowering the edge rather than controlling the center, and designing systems that invite evolution instead of resisting it.

And at the heart of all of this is MEx. Every transformation, whether cultural, technical, or strategic, comes down to how individuals engage with change. Do they feel ownership over the system they're a part of? Do they feel trusted to explore new approaches? Do they feel like their curiosity is rewarded, not shut down? When leadership models MEx thinking—prioritizing individual employee needs (ME) while building enterprise capabilities that scale learning and innovation—transformation accelerates across the organization. If the answer to any of those questions is yes, you've built a *learning* company. And in today's environment, that may be the most important kind of enterprise you can lead.

Trust by Design

The most effective leaders are beginning to see AI not as an alternative to human judgment, but as an enabler of it—an intelligent copilot that accelerates awareness, highlights patterns, and expands the field of view. This is a partnership that changes what becomes possible.

But trust doesn't arrive on day one. In every company I've worked with, confidence in AI has emerged through consistent exposure to meaningful, low-risk outcomes. The journey starts small, beginning where the cost of error is manageable, the data is relatively clean, and the outcome can be validated quickly. Think about demand forecasting, fraud detection, or loan approvals. These use cases are grounded in clear objectives and measurable results, which makes them ideal candidates for early trust-building.

In one financial services client, the AI system wasn't introduced with a headline or a major campaign. It was deployed quietly, behind the scenes, to identify anomalies in customer data. It flagged inconsistencies in how addresses were formatted across multiple internal systems—minor mismatches that, when left unchecked, led to failed approvals and unnecessary friction. The AI applied fuzzy logic to reconcile the records, improving match accuracy and unlocking more accurate customer validation. The result meant more customers were approved for loans they deserved. Employees were freed from reviewing cases that never should have been escalated in the first place. The business saw measurable lift. That's how trust begins, by improving something that matters and showing the result.

When used well, AI delivers what I call an unfair advantage. It grants access to patterns and signals that a person wouldn't have spotted manually, at least not in time to act on them. In one case, a leader described how AI helped surface market insights that would have taken months to extract through manual analysis. In minutes, the system pulled data from fragmented sources, cut through the noise, and revealed opportunity areas the team had overlooked. Those insights didn't make the decision for them, but they did equip the decision-maker with context they hadn't seen before. That's the leverage point. AI makes leaders faster, better informed, and more confident in the steps they take.

Successful teams don't rely on the tools alone. They pair AI-driven insights with human ownership. This combination drives the kind of decisions that move businesses forward, not because they're faster, but because they're smarter. At a risk management group inside a large enterprise, the team built a dashboard that visualized millions of data points in near real time. The AI monitored market activity, geopolitical shifts, and operational signals to surface emerging threats and opportunities. The team didn't turn the dashboard into an autopilot. They used it to sharpen their analysis and respond with speed. The result: a measurable drop in exposure and a more agile response to risk.

Patterns like this matter. They reinforce a strategic truth that too often gets overlooked: Trust in AI grows with use, but only when the use is intentional, transparent, and grounded in impact. These wins build the credibility needed to expand into more critical applications.

Patterns like this matter. They reinforce a strategic truth that too often gets overlooked: Trust in AI grows with use, but only when the use is intentional, transparent, and grounded in impact.

This also changes how we think about leadership. The best leaders don't wait for their teams to be convinced. They curate experiences that prove what the technology can do and build shared understanding by involving the people who will use the tools, not just the ones who built them. And they ensure that humans remain in control, especially when the stakes are high.

The road to trust is paved with design choices. Choose systems that explain their recommendations and problems that are meaningful, yet manageable. The confidence you need won't come from a keynote or a strategy memo. It comes from watching the machine get it right—consistently, reliably, and at a pace that makes you realize just how much more your team can accomplish.

AI as MEx Architect

Every brand is competing to be easier, faster, more relevant, and more helpful. And increasingly, the difference between a good experience and a great one comes down to whether a customer feels known, anticipated, and cared for. This is where AI delivers its most meaningful impact: as an architect of intelligent, proactive experiences.

Rather than reacting to customer needs as they arise, leading organizations are designing systems that can sense those needs ahead of time. AI makes that shift possible because it can analyze subtle behavioral cues, detect patterns, and identify moments of friction before the customer ever raises their hand. When applied strategically, this ability transforms support models from reactive to predictive and turns moments of potential churn into opportunities for lasting loyalty.

One major telecommunications provider faced a recurring challenge with customer churn. Their initial approach involved a reactive support team that intervened only after a customer signaled dissatisfaction. That process worked, but only partially. And often too late. After implementing an AI-powered churn prediction engine, the organization began identifying at-risk customers weeks before they voiced concerns. This early signal enabled the team to reach out proactively with personalized solutions, from billing adjustments to service upgrades. The result was a double benefit: Churn rates declined and customer satisfaction climbed. What had been a firefighting function became a loyalty engine.

In financial services, similar patterns are emerging. One bank used AI to analyze spending behavior, transaction histories, and seasonal trends to detect customers at risk of overdrawing their accounts. Instead of waiting for the problem to occur, the system proactively suggested budgeting tips, nudged users with timely reminders, and even offered personalized product recommendations based on financial goals. These interventions reframed the relationship with MEx. Customers began to see the bank not as a transactional platform but as a partner in their financial well-being.

Across sectors, the same principles apply. In wellness platforms, intelligent systems monitor sleep patterns and activity levels to provide timely guidance on rest and recovery. In B2B environments, predictive analytics flag potential operational issues before they escalate, enabling suppliers to prevent delays and protect business continuity. Each of these experiences reflects a deeper understanding of the individual, their needs, and the context in which they operate.

At the heart of these capabilities is a concept I often call "frictionless loyalty." It's the idea that trust is earned not through grand gestures but through small, consistent moments of value delivered with care. A customer feels loyal when they experience fewer headaches, faster answers, and smarter interactions. They stay not because of points or perks but because the brand understands them better each time they engage. And most importantly, because the brand continually removes obstacles that once felt unavoidable.

Trust is earned not through grand gestures but through small, consistent moments of value delivered with care.

This kind of loyalty is hard to replicate, and harder still to disrupt. It creates a moat around your customer relationships, not by locking people in, but by creating an experience so fluid that switching becomes inconvenient. Competitors may offer similar products, but they can't easily copy the history of interactions, preferences, and context that your system has accumulated over time. That knowledge, when used wisely, becomes a powerful differentiator.

Designing for proactive value also requires rethinking what support looks like. Instead of building larger customer service teams, organizations are embedding intelligence into the flow of every interaction. A well-timed suggestion on a mobile app, a dynamic UI that adapts to past behavior, or a predictive alert before something goes wrong—these are the new markers of thoughtful service. They don't require a customer to ask for help. They eliminate the need for help *in the first place.*

AI allows you to meet your customer not just where they are but where they're going. It invites you to anticipate needs before they become problems and to design experiences that evolve with the individual over time. When applied with care and creativity, it transforms every interaction into a moment of affirmation: You are seen, your time matters, and your experience has been built with you in mind.

Invisible Intelligence

The most powerful advancements in AI often don't announce themselves. They don't arrive with a big unveiling or a change in branding. They emerge in the background, woven into the flow of daily work, making everything feel simpler, faster, and more personal. This is the essence of invisible intelligence—designing systems that anticipate needs, reduce friction, and adapt to the person on the other end, quietly and intuitively.

When AI is used well, the experience doesn't feel more technical; it feels more human. Think of a banking app that doesn't just track your balance but learns your spending habits and offers actionable suggestions that match your goals. There's no dramatic moment of realization. But over time, the user feels more supported, more capable, and more in control.

One of the most promising design patterns behind this kind of support is what I call morphing UI. Instead of presenting the same interface to every user, these systems adjust dynamically based on intent, behavior, and context. If a customer logs in repeatedly to check a loan status, that action moves to the top of their dashboard. If an employee handles a certain type of task more often than others, the tools they need begin surfacing automatically. These subtle changes remove unnecessary steps, save time, and increase the sense that the experience was built with intention.

This same principle shows up in predictive interactions. A well-designed AI system can infer what someone is likely to do next and meet them *there*. In a CRM platform, for example, that might mean pulling up the most recent customer communications the moment an account executive clicks on a contact. In an internal knowledge portal, it could mean surfacing relevant documentation based on a pattern of recent queries or tickets. These are not huge leaps in capability. But they are huge gains in usability. Each one saves a few clicks, a few seconds, and a few mental switches. And those savings compound.

Employee enablement plays a major role in this transformation. When AI helps your team get to what they need faster, with fewer distractions, the entire organization benefits. A service agent no longer wastes time navigating legacy systems to find a customer's history. A marketer receives campaign performance insights without waiting on a weekly report. A product manager spots a shift in usage trends before the support tickets start piling up. These improvements often begin as internal efficiency gains, but they ripple outward into the customer experience.

Small enhancements, executed consistently, have an outsized impact. A shift in tone that makes a notification feel personal instead of generic. A message that arrives at the right time instead of inter-rupting a busy moment. A recommendation that actually reflects someone's past behavior instead of being the result of a broad segmen-tation model. These details can feel trivial in isolation, but together, they create the feeling that this system, this brand, and this interaction were built for ME.

Invisible intelligence restores attention. It frees up people to focus on the parts of their job, or their life, that matter most. Instead of spending energy navigating technology, they spend it making decisions, building relationships, or taking action. The tools fade into the background, and the experience becomes the focus.

This is the future of interface design, and it's already taking shape across industries. In healthcare, AI-powered portals personalize care instructions and appointment follow-ups based on patient history. In e-commerce, platforms adjust product displays and checkout flows based on purchase patterns and predicted preferences. In enterprise tools, task flows adapt to individual roles, surfacing the insights and actions most likely to move the work forward.

The most effective uses of AI won't always be the most visible. They will be the ones that blend seamlessly into the day-to-day, reducing the invisible costs of time, frustration, and rework that slow progress and erode trust.

Working Backward to Leap Forward

Some of the most expensive product failures I've seen didn't collapse because of technical flaws. They failed because they were designed for a customer that didn't exist. They were launched based on internal excitement instead of external demand. And they often had more features than signals.

The antidote is simple, but not easy: Work backward.

This principle, established in chapter two, remains the most reliable compass for building with AI. The starting point is never the technology itself. It begins with a real customer, a clear problem, and a practical understanding of how that person experiences the world. When teams begin with what matters most, they avoid the trap of creating clever solutions in search of a problem.

That foundation has to be supported by alignment. A product built with AI introduces a new set of expectations—about how it works, how it learns, and how it supports decision-making. Without early agreement from stakeholders about what the system will and won't do, the team inherits a recipe for confusion. When an AI-powered feature performs well but misses the mark because it didn't match someone's assumptions, that's not a product problem. It's a leadership one.

The most effective safeguard against that kind of misalignment is assumption validation. Every team walks into a project with some version of "We think this will work." The key is to test that belief before building a full solution. In my experience, this often comes down to making a choice between a prototype and a signal.

A few years ago, I saw two teams approach a similar challenge in very different ways. One group spent weeks building a beautifully designed prototype. The other added a single button to an existing page. The button didn't do anything yet, but it tracked how many people clicked it. That simple act gave them real data. Customers were interested. Engagement was high. And that evidence gave the team the confidence to invest.

The other group had a better-looking demo but no proof of demand. They had built something elegant. The challenge was that no one had asked for it. That lesson still sticks with me; it's not about reducing ambition but about earning the right to build more by testing less.

This lean approach is especially valuable in constrained environments such as small businesses. In those contexts, time and attention are even more limited. The right AI product doesn't overwhelm users with options. It acts as a creative partner that extends their capacity. Think of a local business owner who needs to launch a marketing campaign. Instead of asking them to pick from dozens of templates, the system prompts them for a sentence. "I'm opening a coffee shop in Austin." From there, the AI builds a complete campaign, with tailored copy and timing. It's suddenly a collaborator, not a toolkit.

That kind of partnership only works if the customer understands how the system got there. Which brings us to the final point: explainability. When an AI tool surfaces a recommendation, the output needs to come with a reason. Not just a score but a sentence. This product was suggested because it matches your past purchases. This loan wasn't approved because the debt-to-income ratio exceeded the threshold. These explanations make the system trustworthy. They keep customers engaged and help organizations meet regulatory expectations without sacrificing usability.

Opaque AI doesn't scale. When people don't understand why something happened, they assume the system is wrong. That reaction erodes trust, and trust is the most expensive thing to rebuild.

As AI becomes a core part of product development, the challenge is no longer about whether we can build it. It's about how we design systems that people want to use, can learn from, and trust over time. That means working backward with discipline and treating AI as a creative, explainable, and purpose-built partner.

When we do that, we don't just avoid wasted investment. We unlock a new way to build faster, smarter, and far more aligned with the customers we serve.

Modernization Is a System You Build, Not a Feature You Add

Modernization begins with intent, not with technology. It takes shape in how leaders think, how teams work, and how systems evolve. Throughout this chapter, the clearest pattern has emerged: Progress stalls when organizations try to speed up old systems, and progress accelerates when they choose to redesign how value is created.

The most resilient companies are defined by their willingness to challenge long-held assumptions. They move from linear processes to connected systems, from rigid roles to shared accountability, from perfection to learning velocity. They empower teams at the edges. They design for flexibility. They build architectures that invite change.

AI brings new power to this equation, but it does not change the fundamental truth. Modern systems win when they integrate human judgment with intelligent automation, when they personalize value at scale, and when they build trust step by step. Trust in the data. Trust in the process. And trust in how decisions are made.

To assess where you're at today, you can find another self-assessment, The Innovation Aptitude Quiz, in my Insights Hub by scanning this QR code.

The path forward belongs to the organizations that build momentum one intelligent move at a time. They simplify before they scale and experiment before they invest. They prioritize explainability over mystery and clarity over complexity. And they never lose sight of the human ME—customers, employees, and partners who experience the impact of every decision.

Modernization is a choice to build systems that continually learn. And once that choice is made and modeled from the top, transformation stops being a project and becomes a permanent advantage.

FIVE STEPS TO TAKE NOW

Modernization isn't just about deploying new technologies. It's about rethinking systems, rewiring culture, and reclaiming speed. These five steps offer a practical path from insight to execution, designed to help you lead transformation with clarity, alignment, and momentum.

Step 1: Find Your Cracked Chassis

Identify one core process in your organization that consistently underperforms despite repeated efforts to optimize it. Gather a small cross-functional group and ask:

- What assumptions are baked into how this process operates?
- Where do handoffs break down?
- What would it look like if we built this from scratch for today's customer?

This is your opportunity to shift the conversation from improvement to reinvention, starting with the system, not just the symptoms.

Step 2: Surface the Silent Costs

Quantify one hidden cost of legacy systems, whether it's technical debt, decision latency, or talent attrition due to outdated tools. Work with your teams to estimate:

- Hours lost to rework or manual reconciliation
- Time delays in launching or iterating
- Churn risk from employee frustration

Even directional data helps build the case for change. You don't need perfect math, just enough signal to see where inertia is dragging performance.

Step 3: Redefine Success Around Learning Velocity

Audit one initiative—past or present—through the lens of learning. Ask the team:

- What assumptions did we test?
- What did we learn, and how fast?
- How did that learning shape the next step?

This reflection helps shift focus from outputs to insights. When teams understand that success is measured in discovery, not perfection, they move with more confidence—and more creativity.

Step 4: Codify Your Cultural API

Choose one team or function and invite them to define a shared operating language. Focus on:

- Key terms that clarify expectations
- Protocols for decision-making and escalation
- Patterns for asynchronous communication and ownership

When language becomes consistent, coordination improves. You don't need a manifesto, just a few anchors that make autonomy easier and alignment faster.

Step 5: Launch a Modernization Pulse Check

Facilitate a thirty-minute pulse meeting with a mix of leaders and practitioners. Pose three questions:

- Where are we still rewarding process over progress?
- What tool, system, or habit feels most out of sync with how we need to operate today?
- What one small modernization step could remove friction this quarter?

This exercise creates visibility, signals leadership intent, and empowers teams to take action. Big change often starts with small, visible wins.

PART V

EMBEDDING INNOVATION IN YOUR DNA

CHAPTER TEN

CHAMPIONING CHANGE FROM THE TOP

You don't transform organizations. You transform people.
And then people transform organizations.

—VOLKER HIRSCH

> **Your Mission Possible Blueprint:** Transformation begins when senior leaders stop delegating change and start modeling it. This chapter reframes modernization as a cultural act, not just a systems upgrade. It's your blueprint for leading from the front, removing friction, and rewiring how belief, behavior, and momentum cascade through the organization.

WE'VE ALL HEARD the stories of massive, multimillion-dollar digital transformation initiatives that promise to reinvent the business only to fade into obscurity, leaving behind a few unused servers and an expensive slide deck. In my experience, the biggest lie we tell ourselves about technology is that we're only one platform away from greatness.

The truth is, the real shift doesn't happen in a new application or a redesigned homepage. It shows up in the quiet moments when behavior changes. When culture moves. When what people prioritize, measure, and talk about starts to reflect a different way of working.

I remember sitting with the CEO of a legacy industrial manufacturer. The business had been losing ground to faster, leaner startups. He had poured millions into new software platforms—CRM, analytics, automation. But none of it was translating into growth. He leaned back in his chair, frustration written across his face, and said, "We've spent millions on new technology, and now we're just faster at being wrong than ever before."

It wasn't a speed problem. It was a friction problem.

The company had invested in tools. What it lacked was clarity. When we began the transformation effort, we didn't start with a systems integration road map. We started with a single question rooted in MEx thinking: *What is the simplest, most frictionless way for a customer to get a quote?* This MEx lens—individual relevance plus enterprise capability—became our North Star.

The answer revealed a process so broken, so convoluted, that it took five separate handoffs and an average of four weeks for a prospect to receive a basic price. Customers weren't abandoning them because of product quality. They were leaving because the path forward was too difficult to navigate.

The CEO gave a small, cross-functional team permission to solve just that one issue. No massive rollout. No sweeping change program. Just one concrete pain point. The team built a lightweight internal tool that aggregated the data needed and enabled sales reps to generate quotes in less than two days.

Within a year, that simple fix drove a 30 percent increase in new customer acquisition. This went far beyond a win. This was a catalyst.

That success created a new kind of momentum. The CEO started using a new phrase: *Find the friction.* It became a rallying cry across the business. Everywhere a process created drag, someone raised their hand. Each new solution built on the energy of the last. They were removing barriers, one by one.

Here's what that looked like in action:

- **Manufacturing floor:** They deployed IoT sensors to monitor machine health in real time. Instead of reacting to breakdowns, maintenance became proactive and scheduled. Unplanned downtime dropped 40 percent. More importantly, frontline workers gained control. The job shifted from firefighting to forecasting—less stress, more strategy.
- **Supply chain:** A cloud-based inventory tracker replaced a patchwork of spreadsheets and outdated systems. With one real-time view, managers cut excess stock by 25 percent and fulfilled orders faster. The supply chain lead no longer needed to guess. They had visibility and confidence.
- **Customer service:** They trained an AI model on historical tickets to handle repeat questions. This didn't eliminate the service team—it elevated them. Agents focused on the nuanced, high-value cases where empathy mattered. Customer satisfaction rose by over 15 percent, not because the tech got smarter, but because the human ME was able to deliver better, faster support.

This is how transformation really works. Not as a single top-down command, but as a series of small, undeniable wins that shift belief, behavior, and momentum. One solved problem builds trust. That trust powers the next move. Over time, these shifts accumulate into something much bigger than the sum of their parts.

This is a classic snowball effect. They didn't try to roll out a company-wide transformation from the top down. They found one small, winnable battle, celebrated the success, and used that momentum to build a series of small, incremental victories that ultimately transformed the entire business from the ground up.

The CEO didn't try to force change from the corner office. He acted as a storyteller, bringing clarity, energy, and consistency to the journey. He looked for momentum. When the team delivered a breakthrough in their quote-to-cash process, he didn't just acknowledge it; he amplified it.

He turned that win into a parable, sharing it in town halls and one-on-one meetings, using it as a mirror to reflect what progress looked like in action. He created the conditions for his team to think creatively, take smart risks, and move fast without fear of failure.

That cultural shift was visible in the numbers. Employees began submitting three times as many innovation ideas. Product teams began moving faster, shipping new features in half the time. The pace of change increased, not because he demanded it but because he built an environment where it felt safe and energizing to contribute. In that context, the leader ME is a cultural architect, shaping the norms and values that guide everyone else forward.

In contrast, some transformations stall under the weight of a different leadership approach—one that prizes control over curiosity. I've worked with executives who assumed their job was to issue precise orders, expect perfection, and manage transformation like a battle plan. They held teams to rigid outcomes, discouraged iteration, and prioritized predictable results above shared learning.

These leaders tended to focus on quarterly earnings calls, not customer insights. They pushed for efficiency without making room for discovery. The result was a culture where employees hesitated to experiment. People did what was expected but rarely more. Creativity slowed and momentum vanished.

This isn't an edge case. In my experience, more than 75 percent of failed transformation efforts stem not from technical limitations, but from a lack of leadership buy-in and a deep fear of failure inside the organization. It's what I often refer to as the broken windows effect—small, ignored cracks in the culture eventually widen into systemic paralysis.

The alternative begins with mindset. In TalentLMS' landmark October 2024 *Growth Mindset in the Workplace* report, researchers surveyed three hundred business leaders and one thousand employees across the United States, finding that a strong majority of respondents recognized the positive impact of growth mindsets. In fact, 64 percent of senior executives from organizations that had strong growth mindset cultures observed increased productivity and performance, with 54 percent reporting improved employee engagement.[17] The distinction is in how leaders approach uncertainty. Growth-minded leaders lean into challenges, welcome uncomfortable feedback, and treat setbacks as essential steps in the learning process.

This creates a self-reinforcing loop. The most capable people seek out environments where they're encouraged to think, test, and evolve. The best ideas emerge when risk is respected, not feared. And the organization gains a new kind of strength, one rooted in resilience, flexibility, and forward energy.

---

17   TalentLMS, *Growth Mindset in the Workplace* (TalentLMS, 2024), https://www. talentlms.com/research/growth-mindset-workplace-report.

THE SELF-REINFORCING LOOP
OF A GROWTH MINDSET

Growth-minded leadership makes "everybody wins" inevitable—employees innovate without fear, leaders build organizational resilience that compounds over time, and customers benefit from relentless improvement.

That's the mark of a modern leader. Not someone who commands from the front but someone who cultivates a system that gets smarter with every decision. The leader ME in this scenario isn't just managing performance. They are attracting talent, fostering creativity, and turning transformation into a shared, sustainable practice.

The Tipping Point of Transformation

Leaders who create the right conditions—a safe space for failure, a relentless focus on the human ME, and a clear, compelling story of where they're going—are the ones who enable transformation. They are the connectors who link the technology to the human problem, and in doing so, they don't just transform their company; they transform the people within it. Their success is measured not just in balance sheets, but in the sustained vibrancy and adaptability of the organization itself.

The most successful leaders understand that the company's greatest asset isn't its code or its IP. It's the curiosity, creativity, and courage of the people who show up every day. A leader's job is simply to give others permission to be brilliant.

THE KEY SIGNS OF TRANSFORMATION

Transformation doesn't announce itself with a product launch or a press release. It shows up in the small but unmistakable changes in how people meet, speak, measure progress, take risks, and collaborate across boundaries. A company is truly transformed when these five signals become visible and consistent.

1. The Meeting Room Becomes a Workshop

In a transformed culture, meetings shift from passive reporting to active problem-solving. The agenda is a shared commitment to customer impact. Marketers, engineers, and sales leaders gather around a single unifying prompt: *What's the customer's problem, and how do we solve it together?*

These conversations move faster and dig deeper. They end with experiments to test, not just tasks to assign. The energy in the room shifts. The human ME feels heard and invited to contribute, not just expected to report. At FifthVantage—the innovation consultancy I lead with my fellow Avengers of AI, a team of transformation veterans from companies like AWS and Symantec—we've developed a strategic briefing methodology designed specifically to cut through planning theater and drive rapid, executable decisions. The results speak for themselves: twice as many actionable decisions per meeting and a 50 percent reduction in meeting length without sacrificing outcomes. Our approach equips leaders with the clarity and tools to drive transformation autonomously, delivering measurable ROI in weeks rather than months.

2. The Language Reflects Shared Ownership

Language is often the earliest signal of cultural shift. In organizations that are evolving, teams begin to speak in terms of shared outcomes rather than isolated responsibilities. The phrase "That's not my job" fades out, replaced by a vocabulary centered on customer journeys and end-to-end experience.

Departments begin referencing the same terms, priorities, and protocols. Alignment happens not through heavy-handed coordination but through a common mental model. When teams adopt a unified lexicon, coordination becomes faster and more intuitive. As seen in organizational studies, implementing a shared business language often leads to a measurable acceleration in project delivery and efficiency, demonstrating that removing linguistic and functional barriers is essential for driving business outcomes.[18]

3. The Metrics Prioritize Momentum Over Maintenance

True transformation becomes visible in what an organization chooses to measure and how it responds to those signals. Legacy KPIs such as quarterly revenues remain important, but they're no longer the sole focus. Instead, the spotlight shifts to leading indicators: customer satisfaction, time to value, learning velocity, and employee engagement.

---

18 Joyce Thomas and Deana McDonagh, "Shared Language: Towards More Effective Communication," *Australasian Medical Journal* 6, no. 1 (2013): 46–54, https://doi. org/10.4066/AMJ.2013.1596.

Teams start tracking outcomes that reflect real momentum. They monitor how quickly a customer reaches success, how fast an idea evolves through iteration, and how deeply employees feel connected to their work. This shift brings precision to decision-making and clarity to priorities. By strategically integrating systems that track customer success velocity (NPS, retention) and employee experience (retention, engagement), organizations can achieve significant cross-functional gains, driving the kinds of measurable outcomes consistently demonstrated in transformative organizations.

4. Failure Becomes a Learning Input

In cultures built for change, failure is treated as a moment to extract insight, not assign blame. A team can release a feature that misses the mark and still earn trust because what matters most is what they learn and how quickly they adapt. This mindset is modeled at the top.

I worked with one company where a new initiative fell flat within weeks. Instead of panic or finger-pointing, the CEO gathered the team and asked a single question: What did this teach us? That conversation reshaped the team's confidence. They were challenged to grow instead of being punished.

When failure becomes part of the design, innovation speeds up. Teams experiment more often. Ideas get into the market faster. And the organization gains the resilience to try, learn, and adjust without losing momentum.

5. Structure Gives Way to Network

Transformation thrives in fluid networks, not rigid hierarchies. The org chart may remain for clarity, but the day-to-day collaboration begins to resemble something else entirely, more like a jazz ensemble than a top-down orchestra.

People know their roles, but they also recognize where to flex and when to jump into new conversations. The most valuable connections are often the informal ones, the ones that stretch across functions and flatten the lines of communication.

This networked approach accelerates decision-making and strengthens alignment. Teams stop waiting for permission and start moving based on shared understanding. This shift—mirroring a jazz ensemble, where musicians have clear roles but also the autonomy to improvise—is validated by organizational research showing that networked collaboration and decentralized influence systems are the most effective drivers of decision velocity.[19] The employee ME doesn't have to ask for access. They already have it.

Leadership Isn't Optional

In every transformation I've witnessed, whether a full-blown enterprise overhaul or a targeted digital initiative, there's been one consistent truth: If leadership isn't fully in, the employees won't be either, and the transformation won't succeed. We like to tell ourselves that new technology will be the catalyst. That a shiny new platform or a modern interface will turn the tide. But transformation isn't a software problem. It's a culture problem. And transformation culture, whether we want to admit it or not, starts at the top.

There's been one consistent truth: If leadership isn't fully in, the employees won't be either, and the transformation won't succeed.

19   Scott Sonenshein, "To Adapt During Crisis, Take a Lesson from Jazz," *MIT Sloan Management Review*, January 15, 2024, https://sloanreview.mit.edu/article/to-adapt-during-crisis-take-a-lesson-from-jazz/.

I've seen what happens when it doesn't. When leaders treat transformation as an IT project or a departmental experiment rather than a strategic imperative. You get this noble but frustrating dynamic: Teams pour energy into new tools, reimagined processes, and ambitious ideas, but then you watch them sink under the weight of legacy thinking. It's like trying to turn an ocean liner from a rowboat. You may be paddling furiously, even heroically, but the rudder that actually steers the ship is somewhere else entirely. And without it, all that effort is little more than motion without momentum.

Change that isn't championed by leadership doesn't scale. At best, it survives as a side project. At worst, it becomes a cautionary tale. Because in the absence of a clear and sustained mandate from the CEO and their direct reports, the gravitational pull of "how we've always done it" wins every time.

I've seen this play out time and time again. A CXO might declare that a new initiative is the top priority, then proceed to continue rewarding the same slow-moving behavior that's always been rewarded. They'll say they support innovation, but they'll still expect a fully mapped, risk-free plan. They'll claim they want experimentation, but they'll punish failure. This disconnect is what I call the say–do gap, and it's one of the most corrosive dynamics in any organization. When what leaders say doesn't align with what they do, teams stop listening. Worse, they stop believing.

The solution isn't more strategy decks or top-down mandates. It's modeling the change we expect to see.

I've said it throughout this book, but it bears repeating: One of the most powerful things a leader can do to accelerate transformation is to demystify failure. That means making it not just safe to fail but expected, encouraged, and even celebrated. Because in truly innovative cultures, failure is an input, not an outcome.

I once worked with the CEO of a large financial services company who understood this deeply. He challenged his team to build a new mobile banking app and gave them just one mandate: Launch it in ninety days, even if only one feature works. That was it. No bells. No whistles. Just speed, simplicity, and learning.

And they did it. The first version of the app had exactly one function: Check your balance. But that single feature, delivered fast and without perfection, told them everything they needed to know. It was a huge success, not because it was technologically groundbreaking but because it was anchored in real human need. The team weren't afraid to ship something small, because they knew they wouldn't be punished if the innovation didn't land. That clarity and confidence came from the top.

The CEO lived innovation. He rewarded the act of trying. And as a result, the team began moving faster. They learned more quickly. Within a year, mobile app usage was up by 25 percent. Time to market for new features had improved by 40 percent. And perhaps most importantly, the team didn't just adopt a new tool, they embraced a new mindset.

That's what leadership does. It doesn't just point toward the horizon and say, "Go." It clears the fog and gives permission. It sets the emotional tone of the organization. A leader's behavior isn't just directional, it's contagious.

And that's the real point here: Transformation is a cultural shift, not a tech rollout. And culture cascades. The way leaders speak, the way they make decisions, the way they respond to failure—all of it signals to the rest of the organization what's truly valued.

So if you're a senior leader wondering where to begin, start here: Model what you want others to emulate.

Culture as Code

Modernization begins with the systems that influence how people think, communicate, and work together. Every decision and workflow reflects cultural assumptions that, over time, can become embedded constraints. These patterns are often invisible until they start to limit progress.

In one engagement, with a legacy manufacturing firm, we found that the core issue wasn't technology or process but mindset. The business had been optimized for precision, with success defined by adherence to plan. That model had worked well for decades, but as the market evolved toward speed and flexibility, the organization struggled to adapt. The shift began when we redefined success through learning velocity. Teams were encouraged to experiment, test ideas quickly, and uncover what worked. This created energy across the system and positioned discovery as part of every role.

To support this shift, we focused on full system transparency. Employees gained visibility into how work flowed across functions, which exposed friction points and invited shared accountability. When teams understood the broader context, they moved from isolated roles to co-ownership of the whole.

As collaboration grew, a new challenge emerged: language. Each team had developed its own terminology, shaped by different systems and priorities. This slowed coordination and created confusion. To address it, we implemented a concept called "language as API"—a shared protocol that governed how teams communicated, aligned, and made decisions. It gave everyone a clear interface for coordination without requiring uniformity.

This structure unlocked agility. Teams worked with greater independence while staying connected to the larger mission. The shared language provided clarity, and the system became easier to navigate. The organization gained speed, precision, and coherence by intentionally designing how people interacted.

The shift toward curiosity completed the transformation. People were encouraged to ask questions, test assumptions, and contribute insights. With shared understanding, clear protocols, and visible ownership, the culture evolved into a dynamic system where innovation emerged from the way teams worked together.

This is what it means to treat culture as code. It's the architecture that enables everything else to scale.

From Data Dogma to Evidence-Based Culture

One of the most damaging myths in modern business is that transformation is a matter of tools. Just plug in the AI, fire up the dashboards, and watch the magic happen.

In most companies I've worked with, the issue isn't a lack of data but a lack of insight. There's no shortage of dashboards, databases, and reports. What's missing is the connective tissue between raw information and intelligent action. People don't know where to start. They don't know what to look for. And worse, they don't feel safe asking questions when the data doesn't support the prevailing narrative.

That's where leadership comes in. If the goal is to create a truly modern, high-performing organization, then insight has to become the default language of decision-making. And that shift starts at the top.

There are three classic patterns I see in organizations that claim to be data-driven but aren't.

First, the HIPPO effect—which stands for the *highest-paid person's opinion*. I've seen teams spend weeks analyzing a problem, gathering evidence, and running simulations, only to be overruled in the final meeting by a senior executive who says, "I just don't think our customers want that." No data. No counterpoint. Just instinct. And because of the title, that instinct becomes law. These cultures don't move faster, they move in circles, chasing the preferences of whoever has the loudest voice.

Second, there's the data as justification trap. This is when the data isn't used to discover but to defend. A decision has already been made, and now people scramble to find charts, metrics, or anecdotes to make it look inevitable. It's like watching a lawyer build a case for something they already believe, rather than a scientist exploring what might be true. The end result? You kill the truth. And you teach the organization to mistake confidence for correctness.

And finally, there's the classic line: "We've always done it this way." Often reinforced by what behavioral economists call the IKEA effect—a bias toward overvaluing things we've built ourselves. A system, a process, a way of doing things becomes sacred not because it works but because we made it. It's familiar. It feels safe. But the problem with comfort is that it rarely invites change. And in a world that's shifting as fast as ours, clinging to legacy methods becomes a liability.

The antidote to all of this isn't another analytics platform. It's leadership behavior.

The single most powerful thing a leader can do to build a data-driven culture is to ask better questions, specifically, questions that require evidence. I once worked with a CEO who would pause any discussion that felt like speculation and ask, "Can we back that up with a number?" He didn't do it to intimidate. He did it to create a shared expectation that opinions should be informed, not assumed. And at first, it was uncomfortable. But over time, it built a powerful habit. Teams stopped confusing intuition with insight. People came more prepared. And decisions got better because they were grounded.

I often recommend a simple shift in framing. When the data disagrees with your assumption, don't fight it. Say: "Let's assume the data is right. What hypothesis do we need to test next?" That one shift turns disagreement into discovery and de-escalates tension. And it models the kind of intellectual humility that builds trust.

A great example of this came from an unlikely place: Los Alamos National Laboratory. I was talking to someone there who had access to mountains of historical research and behavioral data but no idea where to begin. It was overwhelming. So we worked backward. Instead of boiling the ocean, we picked one outcome they cared about. Then we traced the data to see what supported it. One small slice. One hypothesis. One insight. And from there, they built momentum.

That's how you scale insight. Not with big bangs or black-box models but with small slices of meaningful evidence. That's how you teach teams to think critically and act confidently. And that's how you break the cycle of gut-feel decision-making masked as strategy.

Here's the core principle: Leaders set the tone. If you reward data fluency, you'll get more of it. If you elevate evidence, you'll see your teams dig deeper. That's how you create an "everybody wins" dynamic. But if you prioritize ego, instinct, or tradition, progress will stall.

The Hidden Costs of Legacy

The biggest risk facing many organizations today isn't market disruption, regulatory complexity, or even AI. It's the quiet weight of legacy systems that no longer serve the speed, scale, or personalization the business requires. This is where so many companies go wrong. They treat modernization as optional—a future-phase initiative, a line item to delay until next year's budget. But the real costs are already here. You just have to know where to look.

I call them the silent killers: agility loss, talent drain, and technical debt. They don't make headlines. They don't show up as clear line items on a balance sheet. But they chip away at performance, culture, and innovation until the organization can't move when it matters most.

The first is loss of agility. When a company is built on rigid processes, siloed decision-making, and monolithic systems, it simply can't pivot with precision. I've seen this play out across industries. A new competitor enters the market with a modular tech stack and agile product strategy. They can iterate in weeks. The legacy player, still burdened by quarterly planning cycles and fragile system dependencies, takes months to respond. Even when the will to move is there, the architecture can't support the shift. And in a landscape where speed is strategy, that gap becomes the wedge that disruptors drive through.

The second killer is a quiet but consistent talent drain. The best people don't want to spend their careers propping up systems from the past. They want to solve meaningful problems using tools that make them more capable. When the internal experience feels clunky, bureaucratic, or outdated, your most capable contributors start to disengage— or they leave. A Qualtrics study found that employees are over 230 percent more engaged and 85 percent more likely to stay beyond three years when they're equipped with the tools and environment to do their job well.[20] That's not a perk. That's a retention strategy.

And then there's the third silent killer: technical debt. This is the accumulation of shortcuts, patches, undocumented workflows, and outdated systems that the business continues to rely on but no longer understands. Every time a team hardcodes a workaround, every time tribal knowledge replaces documentation, every time a legacy system

---

20   Tim Yates, "Is Technology Helping or Hurting Your Employee Retention Efforts?" *MDM Distribution Intelligence*, June 16, 2023, https://www.mdm.com/article/featured/featured-blog/is-technology-helping-or-hurting-your-employee-retention-efforts/.

stays in place "just a little longer," the debt grows. And like any debt, it comes with interest.

McKinsey estimates that up to 80 percent of technology budgets are spent just maintaining outdated systems.[21] That's time and money that could be going toward customer experience, product innovation, or operational scale. Instead, it gets spent keeping the lights on.

These silent costs compound over time. At first, they just slow things down. Eventually, they prevent forward motion altogether. The underlying structure can't handle the velocity being aimed for.

A competitor with clean architecture, cloud-native infrastructure, and decoupled workflows doesn't have to move faster—because they already can. Their agility is built into how their business works. Modern systems architecture creates "everybody wins" conditions: Developers work with tools that enhance productivity, operations teams gain reliability and visibility, and customers experience continuous innovation without disruption.

Leading with Clarity and Consistency

If there's one paradox I keep running into across organizations big and small, it's this: We've never had more ways to communicate, yet we're facing a crisis of clarity. Leaders are speaking louder, sending more emails, hosting more all-hands, but somehow their message still isn't landing. And when a transformation effort lacks clarity, it doesn't matter how hard people work. It's like sending a team onto the field without a scoreboard. They're moving, they're sweating, but they have no idea if they're actually winning.

---

21 Jonathan Godsall et al., "How AI Could Reshape the Economics of the Asset Management Industry," *McKinsey & Company*, July 16, 2025, https://www.mckinsey. com/industries/financial-services/our-insights/how-ai-could-reshape-the-economics-of-the-asset-management-industry.

In times of change, the customer ME craves more than just direction; they crave meaning. Without a clearly articulated why, transformation becomes a series of disconnected tasks. Motivation fades. Alignment splinters. And eventually, momentum stalls.

I've seen this firsthand. At one large global company, the CEO announced a sweeping "customer-centricity" initiative. The vision was compelling. The speech was inspiring. And then ... nothing. No follow-up, no common framework, no shared language. Each department interpreted the mandate in its own way. Marketing launched a new app. Sales rolled out a CRM. Engineering spun up a cloud migration. It was well-intentioned chaos. Like a thousand-piece orchestra with each musician playing a different song. Without a clear, coordinated score, the result wasn't music. It was noise.

That's the danger of ambiguity. A small misdirection at the top, such as a fuzzy message or an undefined goal, cascades into a widespread breakdown in execution. In that case, the organization saw a 30 percent spike in project overlap and a 15 percent decline in cross-functional collaboration. Not because people weren't working hard but because they were working in different directions.

The fix isn't more communication but rather more *meaningful* communication. Alignment is a discipline. A leader's job is to be the bridge over the raging river, not just to hand out more driftwood.

So how do you build that bridge?

1. START WITH THE "WORKING BACKWARD" MEMO

If I could give only one tool to a transformation leader, it would be this. Write a two- to three-page memo that describes the initiative as if it's already complete. What did we do? Who did it help? Why does it matter? This memo isn't fluff. It forces clarity. It strips out the jargon and compels the leader ME to speak plainly in terms of customer value, employee impact, and measurable outcomes.

I worked with a startup that was completely fractured. Each team was building its own road map. Everyone had a different view of the customer. The new CEO came in and said: "No one writes a line of code until we agree on one shared memo describing the customer's problem and how we'll solve it." The resistance was immediate. But the clarity that emerged became their North Star. Once everyone had the same story in their heads, they finally started rowing in the same direction.

2. DEFINE AND MEASURE THE MEx

Transformation doesn't become real until it becomes personal. That means success can't be abstract. It must be experienced by ME across every level of the organization.

For the engineer, success might mean doubling deployment velocity. For the sales leader, it could be a 10 percent reduction in time spent on administrative tasks. For the customer, it might be a 15 percent drop in time to value. When you define transformation in terms of how it helps them, not just the company, you turn a corporate mandate into a personal mission.

3. CREATE A WEEKLY CADENCE OF CLARITY

This might sound simple, but it's one of the most overlooked tools in a leader's arsenal: consistency. Change doesn't land in a single keynote. It takes rhythm. I encourage leaders to create a weekly cadence—whether it's an email, a stand-up, or a short video—where they highlight small wins, surface insights, and remind teams of the why.

One leader I worked with modeled this perfectly. He compared his communication style to that of a fire chief during a crisis.. In the middle of the chaos, he didn't bark orders. He kept his team grounded with calm, regular updates—simple, clear signals that helped everyone stay aligned. The result was a 25 percent lift in employee confidence scores and a 10 percent drop in redundant meetings. People felt much more than informed; they felt anchored.

Ultimately, leading through transformation isn't about having all the answers. It's about becoming the chief storyteller—the one who defines the vision, outlines the path, and celebrates the progress. You're the person who makes the invisible visible. Who makes strategy feel real. And who reminds every ME why their work matters.

When you lead with clarity and consistency, you don't just transform a company. You transform belief. And that's what makes change stick.

Real transformation doesn't begin with technology; it begins with trust. It takes root when leadership stops talking about change and starts embodying it. When clarity replaces confusion, when failure becomes fuel, and when every person in the organization feels essential. The truth is, the biggest lever in any transformation isn't a platform, a dashboard, or a road map. It's a leader willing to go first.

Because when leaders model curiosity, consistency, and courage, they accelerate belief. And belief is what turns momentum into movement. That's your role. That's your opportunity. Not to command from the front but to clear the path, anchor the message, and give your people permission to make the impossible possible.

FIVE STEPS TO TAKE NOW

Modernization means creating the conditions for belief, behavior, and business to shift together. These five steps are designed to help you operationalize the insights from this chapter and turn your transformation intent into sustained, scalable momentum.

Step 1: Find the Friction

Start small. Identify one high-impact process—something critical to your customer or employee experience—that's consistently bogged down by unnecessary complexity, delay, or handoffs. Then gather a cross-functional team and ask:

- Where does this create pain for ME?
- What assumptions are we clinging to that no longer serve us?
- If we rebuilt this for today's world, how would it work?

This isn't about optimizing the old. It's about reimagining from the ground up.

Step 2: Measure the Momentum Killers

Behind every stalled initiative is a hidden cost dragging performance down. It might be technical debt, delayed decisions, or the silent churn of your best people. Don't wait for perfect math; directional data is enough. Ask your teams:

- How much time do we lose to rework, redundant meetings, or outdated tools?

- Where are we prioritizing status updates over forward motion?
- What's the opportunity cost of doing nothing?

Surfacing these invisible costs builds urgency and helps you prioritize where to act next.

Step 3: Model the Behavior You Want to Scale

Choose one visible decision or initiative where you can personally demonstrate transformation in action. This could be:

- Sharing a recent failure and the insight it generated in a public forum
- Asking "What evidence supports this?" in a high-stakes meeting instead of defaulting to intuition
- Publicly championing an experiment that didn't require executive approval

Then reflect with your leadership team:

- What behavior am I rewarding through my own actions?
- Where is my say–do gap widest?
- How can I make my commitment to change more visible and consistent?

Transformation cascades from the top. When leaders model curiosity, humility, and evidence-based thinking, they give permission for the entire organization to follow.

Step 4: Normalize Evidence Over Ego

Culture doesn't become data-driven by mandate. It becomes data-driven through modeling. Start with your own behavior. In your next decision-making forum, ask:

- What evidence supports this?
- Can we frame this as a hypothesis instead of a directive?
- What are we trying to learn—not just build?

Model intellectual humility. Reward evidence over instinct. And make it safe to say, "I don't know, but let's find out."

Step 5: Create a Cadence of Clarity

Don't wait for the next all-hands to drive alignment. Set a weekly rhythm—a short update, a Slack post, a team huddle—where you:

- Highlight small wins that reflect the right behaviors
- Reinforce the why behind the work
- Ask where teams feel friction or confusion

Clarity doesn't scale by accident. It scales through repetition, visibility, and emotional resonance.

CONCLUSION

DIGITAL TRANSFORMATION IS a continuous shift in how organizations define value, create momentum, and sustain relevance. At the center of this shift is a fundamental rethinking of success. Traditional indicators—quarterly earnings, operating margins, or shareholder returns—remain important, but they no longer tell the whole story. In a world shaped by speed, complexity, and rising expectations, enduring success is measured by how well an organization adapts to change, learns from its environment, and delivers meaningful experiences that scale.

That redefinition starts with people. Whether it is a customer choosing your product, an employee building your next capability, or a partner aligning to your platform, every signal of progress comes from a human response. Transformation moves when people engage, believe, and act with confidence. Organizations that anchor their strategy in MEx—personalized, intelligent, and intuitive experiences—are better positioned to earn trust, build loyalty, and generate compounding returns.

The best indicators of progress are often invisible at first. You see them in the way teams begin to share insights across functions, in how frontline employees feel empowered to solve problems in real time, and in how customers respond with repeat engagement instead of reactive churn. These signals point to a new kind of performance, one that favors agility, shared learning, and continuous reinvention. When the conditions for curiosity, speed, and simplification are embedded into daily work, the organization begins to run differently.

This reframing also expands the role of technology. It is no longer a support function but a strategic capability, woven into the operating model and infused into how decisions are made. The companies that grow sustainably are those that treat data as infrastructure, automation as a performance multiplier, and AI as an enabler of human creativity.

What defines success today is clarity of purpose and the ability to move with direction and precision. Not because every decision is perfect but because each one is aligned with a broader vision, guided by real-time insight, and executed by teams that know how to learn and adapt. That is the new foundation for growth. And it's one every leader can begin building, no matter where they are in the journey.

The Role of the Modern Leader

Modernization demands leadership that knows how to build conditions for discovery, resilience, and momentum. In today's environment, authority alone doesn't move the organization forward. What matters is a leader's ability to shape the environment where curiosity thrives, where people feel safe to explore, and where teams are empowered to act on what they learn.

The most effective leaders are culture designers. They understand that strategy succeeds only when people are willing to engage with uncertainty and move with clarity. These leaders do not view change as disruption to be managed but as energy to be harnessed. They prioritize systems that support experimentation and make it safe to question assumptions. In these environments, learning becomes a strategic capability, not an afterthought.

Psychological safety is the foundation for this kind of leadership. When teams feel safe to surface problems, admit gaps in knowledge, or suggest new approaches, they contribute more fully. Ideas travel farther. Risks are flagged earlier. And decisions benefit from broader insight. High-performing cultures are rarely the result of strict oversight. They emerge when people know that accountability is shared, not feared.

Leadership today also requires a commitment to capability building. New tools and platforms only accelerate transformation when people are equipped to use them with confidence. Leaders who invest in digital literacy, data fluency, and agile ways of working signal to the organization that growth is an ongoing process. They model learning in public, ask better questions, and invite others to shape the solution, not just execute the task.

What distinguishes modern leadership is not charisma or control, but repeatable behavior that fosters trust, velocity, and shared ownership. This includes clear priorities, transparent decision-making, and the ability to translate vision into action. Leaders who create alignment between strategy and everyday work eliminate unnecessary friction and unlock forward motion.

The role of the modern leader is to build the scaffolding that supports evolution. That means designing operating models that encourage iteration, reinforcing habits that accelerate insight, and staying present in the details without micromanaging the process. In this kind of environment, transformation becomes the natural output of a culture designed to adapt.

Mindsets That Matter for the Future

Sustained transformation begins with the way leaders think. Strategy, tools, and road maps all matter, but mindset is what determines whether an organization evolves or stalls. As the pace of change accelerates, the most important asset a leader can cultivate is a set of mental models built for adaptability, clarity, and long-term value creation.

The first mindset is working backward from the customer. This principle keeps the focus anchored in real-world outcomes. It disciplines teams to define success not by features shipped or systems deployed but by the clarity of the problem being solved. When customer value shapes every decision, technology becomes a tool for relevance above all else. This mindset ensures that product design, service delivery, and internal processes are shaped around the lived experiences of the people they serve.

Another essential mindset is treating data as infrastructure. Data is the foundation for precision, personalization, and intelligent automation. Leaders who build their strategies on clean, consistent, and well-governed data lay the groundwork for agility at scale. They create environments where insight flows to the edge and empowers faster, smarter decisions across the enterprise.

Resilience also begins in our mindset. In times of complexity or disruption, what enables teams to respond effectively is their ability to simplify, to trust in their systems, and to move at a sustainable pace. Resilience means designing ways of working that flex under pressure. Simplicity eliminates friction. Trust reduces drag. Speed creates momentum. Leaders who internalize this operate with intentionality, reducing noise while amplifying what matters most.

These mindsets become even more powerful when practiced consistently. They inform how meetings are run, how goals are set, how investments are prioritized, and how success is measured. And they shift the organization's energy away from reacting and toward shaping the future.

What Comes Next?

The next wave of transformation won't be defined by a single breakthrough. It will emerge through the convergence of intelligent systems, modular architectures, and increasingly adaptive interfaces all working together to reduce friction, unlock new forms of value, and anticipate what people need before they ask.

AI-as-copilot is quickly becoming a standard across domains. From sales and customer service to product development and financial forecasting, intelligent agents are enhancing the work of individuals by surfacing insights, automating repetitive tasks, and accelerating analysis. These tools are not meant to replace human thinking but to extend it. When designed thoughtfully, they allow people to focus on higher-order problems, creative strategy, and decision-making at speed.

Intelligent interfaces are evolving from static dashboards into dynamic experiences that sense user intent and respond to context. This shift makes technology feel more human and less transactional. Interfaces adapt based on behavior, adjust based on history, and evolve as relationships deepen. Whether embedded in mobile apps, internal tools, or customer portals, these systems are increasingly defined by what they know about the individual and how effectively they can act on that knowledge.

Predictive automation represents another leap forward. By analyzing patterns across large volumes of data, organizations can surface signals earlier and respond with precision. This is particularly valuable in operational areas such as inventory management, resource planning, customer retention, and risk mitigation. It allows teams to move from reacting to shaping outcomes in real time.

Underlying all of these advances is a shift toward modular platforms. Rigid, monolithic systems are giving way to architectures that are flexible by design. With API-driven integrations and loosely coupled components, organizations can test, scale, and evolve faster than ever before. This modularity supports a more agile operating model and makes it easier to incorporate emerging capabilities without disrupting the entire system.

As these trends take shape, the imperative for ethical stewardship grows. Each advance brings both opportunity and responsibility. Leaders must ensure that the tools they deploy are transparent, fair, and aligned with their values. Bias must be addressed early. Privacy must be respected by default. And teams must be equipped to understand, interpret, and govern the decisions these systems influence.

What comes next will demand clarity and conviction. The technologies are powerful, but their impact will depend on how intentionally they are applied.

Your Mission Possible Where Everybody Wins

Every transformation starts with the decision to take just one meaningful step forward—one shift in mindset, one improvement to a process, one choice to act with greater clarity. This book was built around the premise that "mission possible" is a practical philosophy for modern leadership.

Throughout these chapters, we've explored the strategies and systems that help organizations build speed, scale, and customer-centered intelligence. But more than that, we've laid out a blueprint for building confidence in your data, in your people, and in your ability to lead through uncertainty with purpose. When teams trust the foundation beneath them, they can move with conviction. When customers feel seen, they stay loyal. When employees are empowered, innovation compounds.

This next chapter belongs to you. Whether your role is in the C-suite, on a transformation team, or leading a product function, the opportunity ahead is clear: Lead with intent. Ask sharper questions. Treat data as a design material. Build for speed and resilience. And most of all, anchor your strategy in the people you serve both inside and outside your organization.

The future favors the leaders who are ready to experiment, ready to listen, and ready to act. You don't need to have every answer before you begin. You just need to start. Make the first change. Open the first conversation. Launch the first test. And then learn fast, share what works, and keep going.

Your Next Step: Architecting Action

If you're looking for guidance on where to begin or how to go further, I invite you to connect with me and the team at FifthVantage (fifthvantage.com). Whether through strategic workshops, keynote sessions, or long-term transformation partnerships, we help organizations turn ambition into execution and build momentum that lasts. Or connect with me directly at mattdomo.com, where you can:

- **Visit The Future Architect:** Explore my latest insights, frameworks, and strategic guidance.
- **Book a Keynote:** Bring battle-tested strategies from the stage to your boardroom.
- **Stay Ahead:** Subscribe to the *Everyone Wins Briefing* for exclusive AI insights and news.

You've seen what's possible. Now it's time to build what comes next.

ACKNOWLEDGMENTS

MY DEEPEST GRATITUDE begins with the people who forged the purpose and resolve that made this book possible.

To my wife, **Kim**, for over twenty-five years of unwavering support, belief, and consistently giving me the space and time to pursue this mission of meaningful change. You are my constant.

To my parents, **Ruthann** and **Rich**. Your love and life lessons taught me the resolve to push boundaries, navigate adversity, and ignore those who said it couldn't be done. That unwavering drive has proven the naysayers wrong countless times, and your influence remains the bedrock of my resolve and my commitment to purposeful action.

I owe a profound debt of gratitude to three key mentors, **Jeanann Honaker, Jeff Alger,** and **David Treadwell**, for challenging me to become the leader I am today. I have benefited both personally and professionally from your invaluable lessons. In your honor, I dedicate myself to upholding the principle of paying it forward and continuing to give back to the community that shaped me.

This book is the product of true collaboration. A heartfelt thank you to the many friends and colleagues who were my sounding board. Phone-a-friend is a real thing, and your consistent dedication and candid feedback refined these blueprints: **Lisa Pistilli, John Powell,**

Kirk Edwards, Sebastian Rivas, Sheri Desmarest, Cagan Sean Yuksel, Mohammed Hajibashi, and **Steve Kearsley**.

Thank you also to **Entrepreneur Books**. You provided a national and global platform to share my story, offering unmatched publishing and marketing services. I value the platform and, even more, the friendships we've built along the way.

Finally, thank *you*. By purchasing this book, you've made a commitment to action against the digital chaos. I deeply admire that resolve, and my hope is that these battle-tested frameworks serve as your ultimate guide, providing the clarity and strategic velocity needed for success.

Now, let's go build your Mission Possible together—so everybody wins.

ABOUT THE AUTHOR

MATT DOMO, Future Architect, transforms complexity into clarity and action. Over his career, he has helped shape some of the most transformative innovations in cloud computing, AI, and digital strategy. As cofounder of Amazon Web Services' Database Division, he helped pioneer cloud computing and laid the foundation for a multibillion-dollar market that redefined how businesses scale and innovate.

Matt's expertise has guided governments, Fortune 500 companies, and universities around the world—including the United Nations, Verizon, HP, Stanford University, and the US Space Force. His leadership has been recognized globally, including being named one of *USA Today's* "Top 5 Visionary Entrepreneurs" and ranked first on MSN's 2025 "Top Ten AI Leaders to Follow," affirming his reputation for creating actionable blueprints that turn disruption into opportunity.

In *Everybody Wins: The Business Leader's Mission Possible Guide to AI Success*, Matt shares his "mission possible" approach to transformation, equipping leaders to reimagine business models, empower teams, and accelerate decision-making with AI-powered insights. His goal is simple: Help organizations stop reacting to disruption and start architecting futures in which everybody wins.

Based in Austin, Texas, Matt is an avid Ohio State football fan, barbecue enthusiast, and music devotee. He lives with his wife and two sons.